HIP TO CROCHET

23 Contemporary Projects for Today's Crocheter

Judith L. Swartz

Editor: Marilyn Murphy
Technical editor: Jean Lampe
Illustrations: Ann Swanson
Photography: Joe Coca
Photo styling: Ann Swanson
Cover and interior design: Bren Frisch
Production: Samantha L. Thaler
Copy editor: Stephen Beal
Proofreader and indexer: Nancy Arndt

Interweave Press Inc.
201 East Fourth Street
Loveland, Colorado 80537-5655
www.interweave.com

Printed in China by Everbest Printing Company

Library of Congress Cataloging-in-Publication Data

Swartz, Judith L., 1953-
Hip to crochet : 23 contemporary projects for today's crocheter / Judith L. Swartz.
p. cm.
ISBN 1-931499-52-7
1. Crocheting--Patterns. I. Title.
TT825.S883 2004
746.43'4041--dc22

2004003762

10 9 8 7 6 5 4 3 2 1

ACKNOWLEDGMENTS

I am very grateful to have had the privilege and challenge of writing this book. However, it would not have materialized without the help of many people. My sincere thanks go out to all who participated. First, to my friend and editor Marilyn Murphy; Once again your vision and hard work have kept me going forward. Your capabilities continue to inspire me, and I treasure being able to work with you again. To Jean Lampe, my technical editor; I am convinced that you have the patience of a saint, the eyes of an eagle, and the mind of a mathematician. I am so grateful that I have been lucky enough again to have the support of your expertise. ■ Thanks to the entire staff at Interweave Press, a talented group of people who have each added their hard work and personal touches to give this book its incredible look. ■ Thank you to all the companies who supplied the beautiful yarns for the projects in this book. It is always a pleasure to work with fine materials. ■ Thanks to my crocheters Lynn Gates and Birgitta Stolpe. I am very grateful for your quick and careful work and your willingness to take on the task. ■ Thank you also to my dear friend Lynn Horwitz Coe for your design consulting expertise as well as your enthusiasm and your belief in me. I must also acknowledge my college crochet teacher, Renie Breskin Adams, who first taught me the versatility and beauty of crochet. ■ I would also like to acknowledge my family. I am very grateful to my wonderful husband, Joel Marcus, for his support, encouragement, love, and patience, and for giving me the time I needed to complete this project. ■ Thank you to my sister Susan Fish for her love and support. Thank you to my parents, Claire and Alex Swartz; though no longer with us, they continue to inspire me. Last of all, I must mention my cat and dog, Charlotte and Tova, who stayed on my lap or by my side, providing their own special style of love and support through many hours of crochet.

TABLE OF CONTENTS

Cozy Bohemian Coat Sweater on page 90

TECHNIQUES AND TIPS

INTRODUCTION

As a fiber major attending college in the 1970s, concentrating on nonloom construction techniques, I found that crochet became a natural form of artistic expression. Ever since those undergrad days, I have valued crochet as a marvelous means of creativity. ■ I value crochet with good reason: It is a very simple technique that is capable of producing very sophisticated results. You need only one simple tool and yarn, and you can easily learn the components because one stitch builds upon the next in complexity. Crochet is astoundingly versatile—you can create the finest of gossamer heirloom lace as successfully as a sturdy jute rug. Given these facts, and considering the vast potential of the technique, you might think that crochet would have an even more devoted following than it already does. ■ For some people, however, the word crochet brings to mind only images of doilies, granny squares, and lumpy sweaters, so they dismiss the technique without ever realizing its beauty. Doilies are charming, even purposeful—but they may well be anachronistic in the twenty-first century. Granny squares were probably invented out of the necessity to use small scraps of yarn, much like patchwork quilts; while they will always serve a purpose, they may still be recovering from overexposure in the 1960s and 1970s. As for crocheted sweaters, they needn't be lumpy. Refined and carefully worked, these sleek new sweaters debunk the fussy, old myth. ■ With crochet's recent surge in popularity, an enthusiastic new generation is eagerly exploring its great potential. In writing this book, I wanted to create designs that represent the crochet of today; however, I've allowed the crocheter's fondness for vintage patterns to help shape designs that are contemporary, yet classic. Today's crocheters easily can construct (but aren't limited to) the projects in *Hip to Crochet*, and while some projects may have roots in the past, they all have a very viable, fun, and fresh purpose in the present. ■ You'll find the patterns, in user-friendly formats, easy to read. Sidebar lessons provide further information and help demystify details. All in all, I hope that this book will inspire the next generation of crochet enthusiasts with a new-millenium approach and a positive learning experience.

BASICS

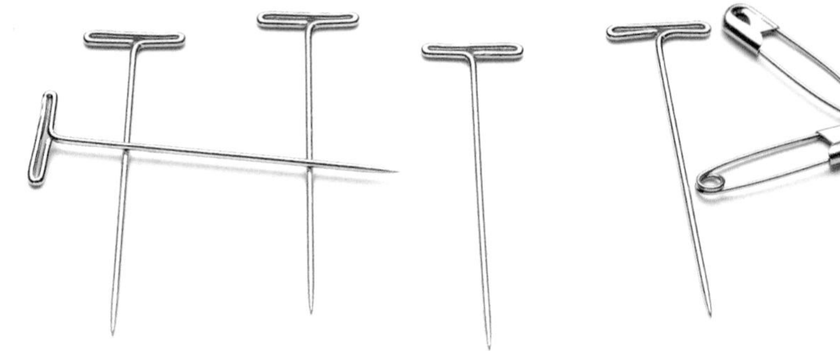

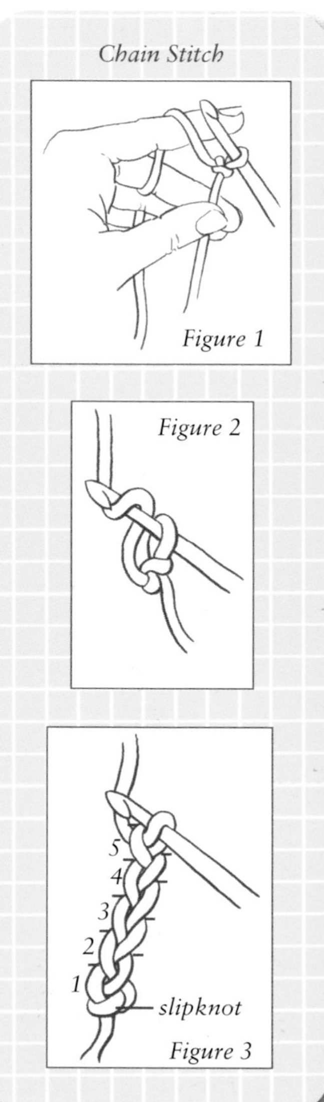

Holding the Hook

There are two ways of holding the crochet hook—pencil style (Figure 1) or knife style (Figure 2). Try them both to see which way is most comfortable for you.

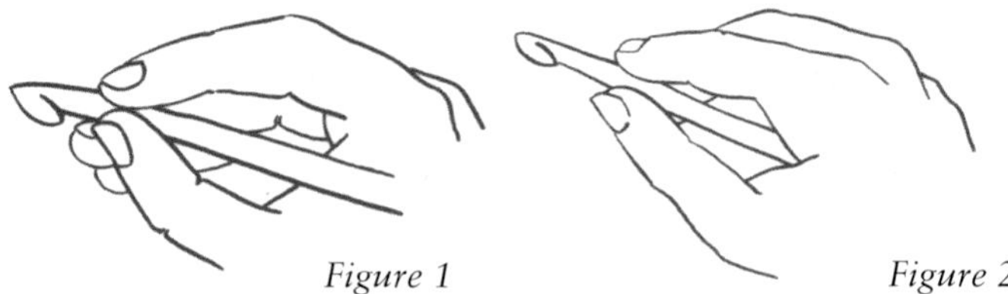

Slipknot

A foundation chain begins with a slipknot. Starting about four to six inches from the end of the yarn, make a loop (Figure 1), put the designated hook through it (Figure 2), and gently pull the end to tighten the loop on the hook (Figure 3). Don't pull the end too tightly or you won't be able to work into this stitch.

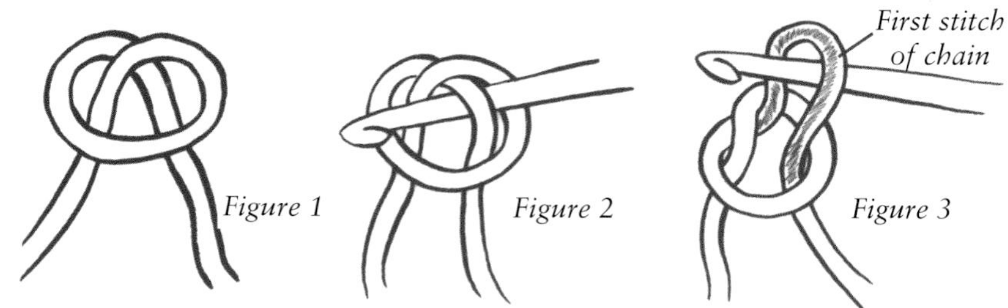

Chain Stitch

The first row of any crochet pattern—often called the foundation chain or row—is worked into a chain stitch. Holding the yarn as shown (Figure 1) in either your right or left hand, insert the hook under then over the yarn on your index finger (Figure 2) and pull the yarn through the loop on your hook. Repeat this step, moving your thumb and forefinger "up" the chain as you work, until the chain is the instructed length (Figure 3). Each loop counts as a stitch. If the pattern instructs you to chain 10 stitches, you will chain 10 plus the number for the *turning chain*.

Turning Chain

The turning chain is the number of chain stitches worked at the end of the row to achieve the required height for the next row of stitches. For *single crochet*, chain one extra stitch; for *half double crochet*, chain two extra stitches; for *double crochet*, chain three extra stitches; for *treble crochet*, chain four extra stitches.

Working Stitches

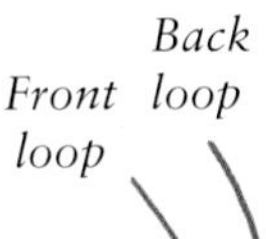

The most common way to hold the chain is with the loops facing you, and inserting the hook under both the front and back loops of the chain (Figure 1). Some patterns may call for you to work into only the front or back loop, or around the post, the vertical bar of the stitch (Figure 2).

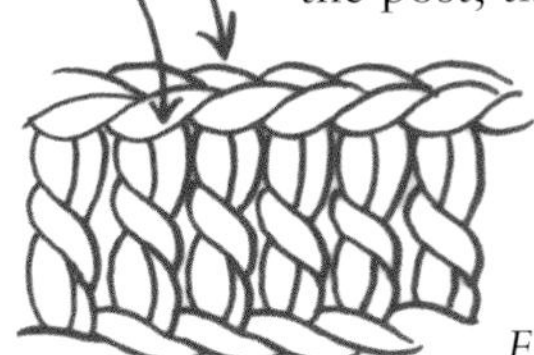

Figure 1

Figure 2

Single Crochet

Make the foundation chain to the instructed length. Then begin the first row:
(Figure 1) Insert the hook through the second chain from the hook.
(Figure 2) Take the yarn over the hook, and bring through first loops (the second chain picked up in step 1).
(Figure 3) Yarn over hook again.
(Figure 4) Draw yarn through both loops on hook. This completes one single crochet. Insert the hook into the next chain and repeat from the second step until the row is complete.
(Figure 5) At the end of the row, chain one for the turning chain, and turn work to begin next row.
(Figure 6) Insert the hook under both top loops of the first single crochet, and beginning from the second step, continue to work one single crochet into each stitch across the row. All following rows are done the same as this row.

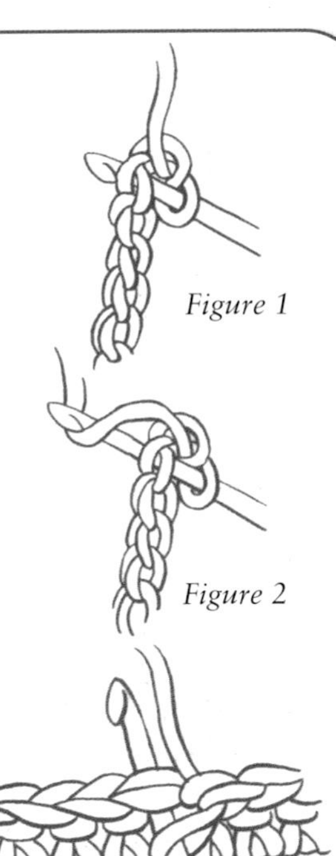

Figure 1

Figure 2

Figure 3

Figure 4

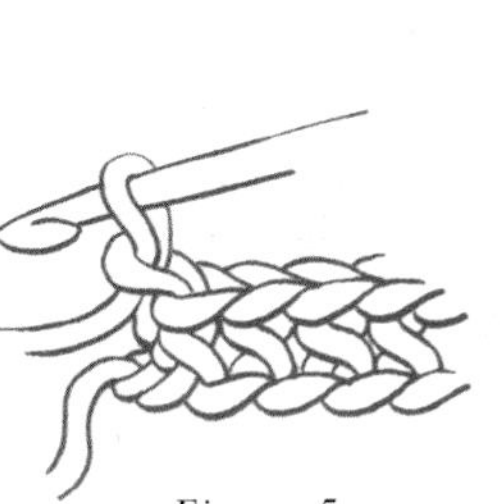

Figure 5

Figure 6

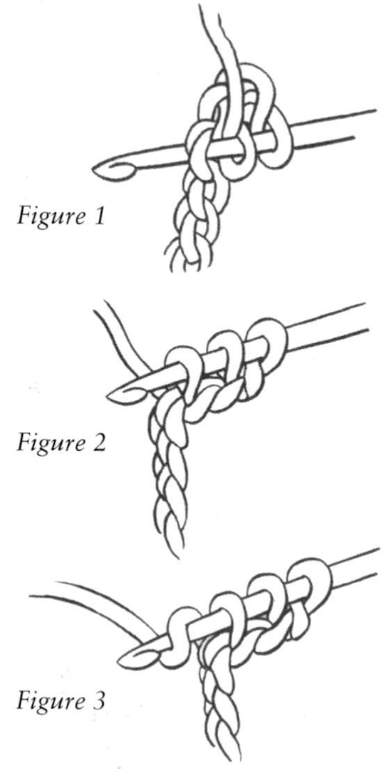
Figure 1
Figure 2
Figure 3

Half Double Crochet

Make the foundation chain to the instructed length. Then begin the first row:

(Figure 1) With yarn over hook, insert the hook through the third chain from the hook.

(Figure 2) Take the yarn over the hook, and bring through the chain—three loops are now on hook.

(Figure 3) Yarn over hook again.

(Figure 4) Draw yarn through all loops on hook. This completes one half double crochet. Yarn over hook, insert the hook into the next chain and repeat from the second step until the row is complete.

(Figure 5) At the end of the row, chain two for the turning chain, and turn work to begin next row.

(Figure 6) Yarn over hook, skip the first stitch, and insert the hook under both top loops of the next stitch, and beginning from the second step, continue to work one half double crochet into each stitch across the row.

All following rows are done the same as this row.

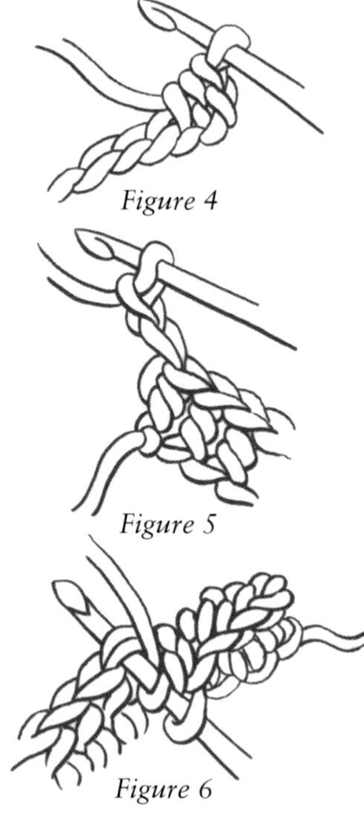
Figure 4
Figure 5
Figure 6

Double Crochet

Make the foundation chain to the instructed length. Then begin the first row:

(Figure 1) With yarn over hook, insert the hook through the fourth chain from the hook.

(Figure 2) Take the yarn over the hook, and bring through the chain—three loops are now on hook.

(Figure 3) Yarn over hook again.

(Figure 4) Draw yarn through first two loops on hook.

(Figure 5) Yarn over hook and draw yarn though remaining two loops. This completes one double crochet.

Yarn over hook, insert the hook into the next chain and repeat from the second step until the row is complete. At the end of the row, chain three for the turning chain, and turn work to begin next row. The turning chain counts as the first double crochet of the next row.

(Figure 6) Yarn over hook, skip the first stitch, and insert the hook under both top loops of the next stitch, and beginning from the second step, continue to work one double crochet into each stitch across the row.

All following rows are done the same as this row.

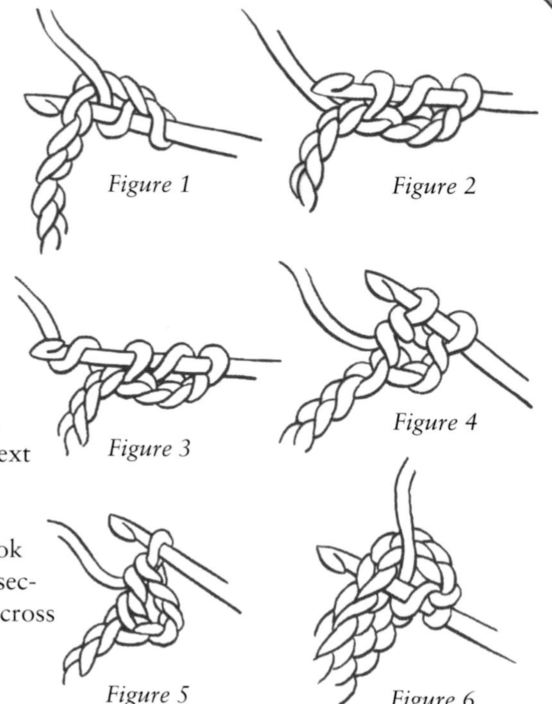
Figure 1
Figure 2
Figure 3
Figure 4
Figure 5
Figure 6

Treble Crochet

Make the foundation chain to the instructed length. Then begin the first row:
(Figure 1) With yarn over hook twice, insert the hook through the fifth chain from the hook.
(Figure 2) Take the yarn over the hook, and bring new yarn through the chain—four loops are now on hook.
(Figure 3) Yarn over hook again and draw yarn through first two loops on hook—three loops are now on hook.
(Figure 4) Yarn over hook and draw yarn through next two loops on hook—two loops remain.
(Figure 5)Yarn over hook and draw yarn through last two loops on hook. This completes one treble crochet.
Insert the hook into the next chain and repeat from the second step, except begin with yarn over hook twice, until the row is complete. At the end of the row, chain four for the turning chain, and turn work to begin next row. The turning chain counts as the first treble crochet of the next row.
(Figure 6) Yarn over hook twice, skip the first stitch, and insert the hook under both top loops of the next stitch, and beginning from the second step, continue to work one treble crochet into each stitch across the row. All following rows are worked the same as this row.

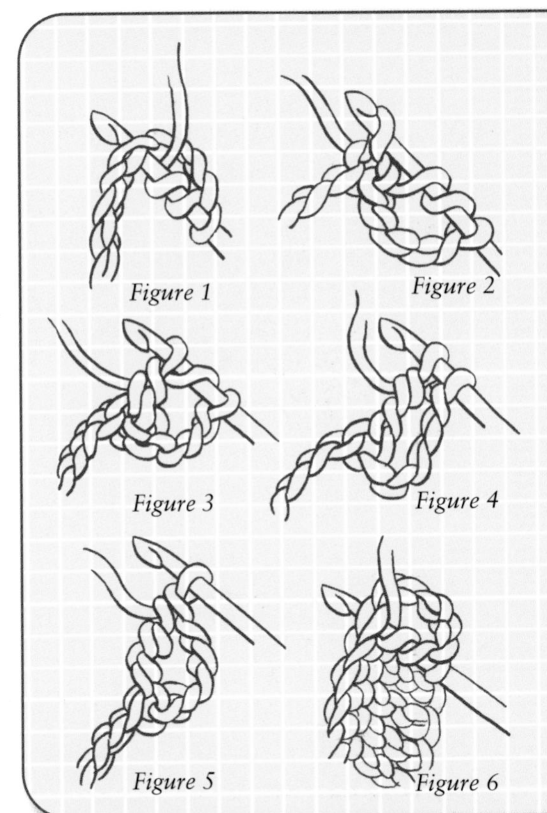

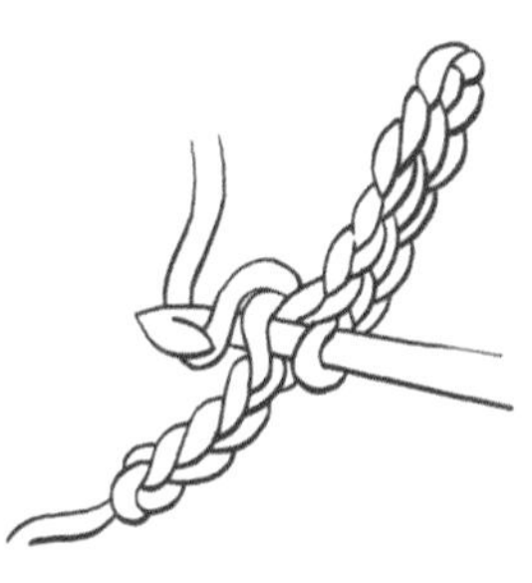

Slip Stitch

Make the foundation chain to the instructed length. Then begin the first row:
Insert the hook into the second chain from the hook, yarn over hook, and pull a loop through the stitch and the loop on the hook. One slip stitch has been worked.
Insert the hook through the next chain and draw the loop through the chain and the loop on the hook. Continue to work a slip stitch across the row (Figure). This makes a nice cord or edging.

WORKING ROWS

A row consists of a group of stitches crocheted from one end of the work to the other. Rows are generally worked from right to left. Count your stitches either as you work or at the end of a row. It's good to double check your stitch count to make sure you haven't unintentionally decreased or increased a stitch.

Decreasing

To decrease is to eliminate one or more stitches. Internal decreases are worked within a row. External decreases are worked at the beginning or end of a row. Instructions are given in the patterns for each particular stitch being worked.
Method I: Simply skip a stitch, working into the second stitch, rather than the next one (Figure 1).
Method II: (Figure 2) Draw a loop through each of the next two stitches, yarn over.
(Figure 3) Draw the yarn through all three loops on the hook. One stitch has been made from the two stitches.

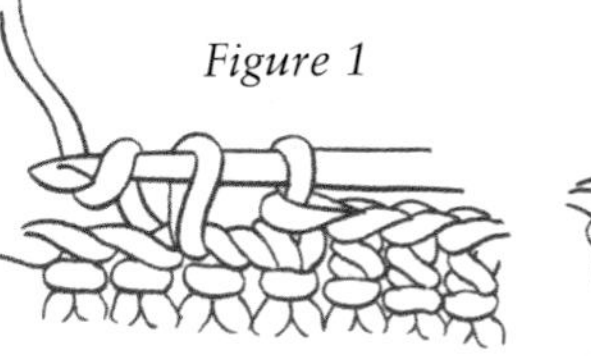

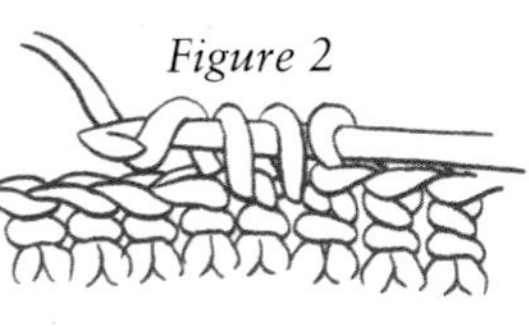

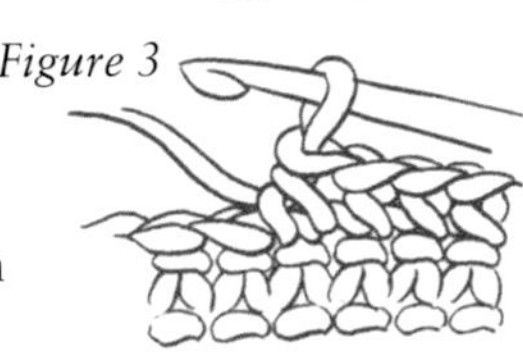

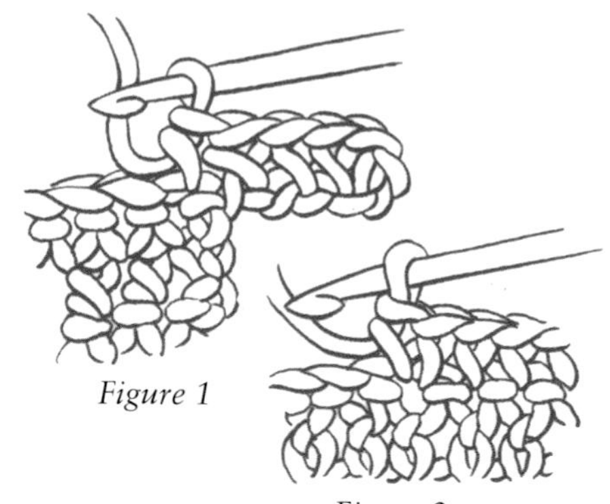
Figure 1

Figure 2

Increasing

To increase is to add one or more stitches. External increases are worked at the beginning or end of a row. Internal increases are worked within a row. Instructions are given in the patterns for each particular stitch being worked.

External: (Figure 1) At the end of the previous row, work one additional chain stitch for each stitch to be increased, plus the number of turning chains. Turn work. Work the pattern stitch into the extra chain stitches and complete the row as usual.

Internal: (Figure 2) The simplest way to increase is to work two stitches into one stitch.

Joining a New Yarn

When making a project that requires more than one ball of yarn or more than one color, you will need to join a new yarn. Joining a new yarn is done either at the beginning of a row or, if working in a color pattern, while working a row. Do not knot the yarns in your work.

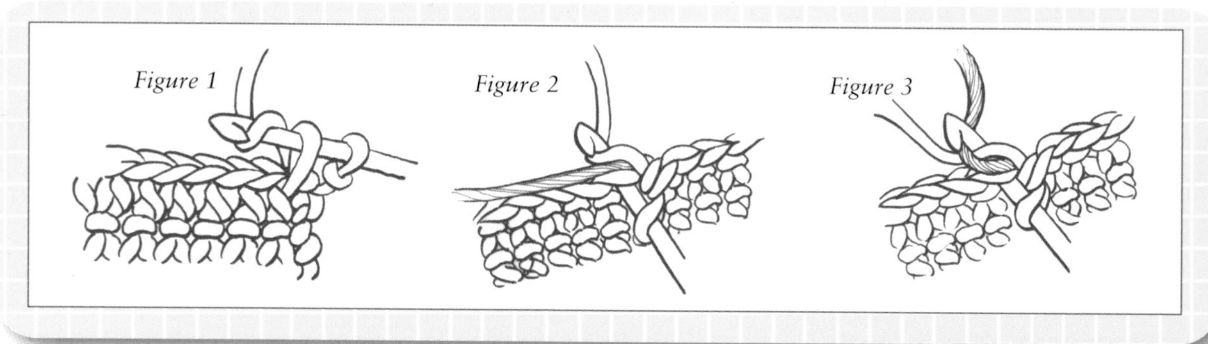
Figure 1 Figure 2 Figure 3

Beginning of row: Fasten off the old yarn. Attach the new yarn with a slipknot to the hook, and start the row with the new yarn (Figure 1). Continue working as usual.

While working a row: (Figure 2) Place the new yarn along the top of the work and crochet a few stitches over the new with the old yarn.

(Figure 3) Change to the new yarn and begin working stitches with the new yarn over the old yarn.

After finishing the piece, work the ends into the wrong side of work.

■ WORKING IN ROUNDS

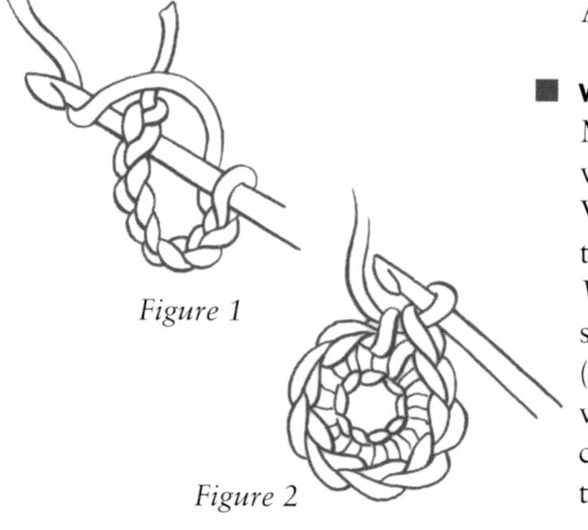
Figure 1

Figure 2

Many patterns start with a foundation chain with a specified number of stitches, where the last chain is joined to the first chain with a slip stitch, forming a circle. When crocheting in rounds you are always working from right to left, without turning the work, and working on the right side.

Version I: (Figure 1) Chain the required number of stitches and join with a slip stitch to form a ring.

(Figure 2) The pattern will then start reading “rounds” instead of “rows.” You will work the pattern stitch into each chain stitch as you would a row and when you come back to the starting place, a round has been completed. Join with a slip stitch to the first stitch.

Version II: (Figure 1) Wrap yarn around your index finger three times.
(Figure 2) Place hook over the end of yarn attached to yarn ball.
(Figure 3) Yarn over and pull through loop on hook.
(Figures 4–5) Continue working single crochet around the two strands until required number of stitches.
(Figure 6) Pull yarn end slightly.
(Figure 7) Pull yarn A, and then pull yarn B and tighten yarn B.
(Figure 8) Tighten yarn A by pulling the end.
(Figure 9) Join with slip stitch to the first stitch.

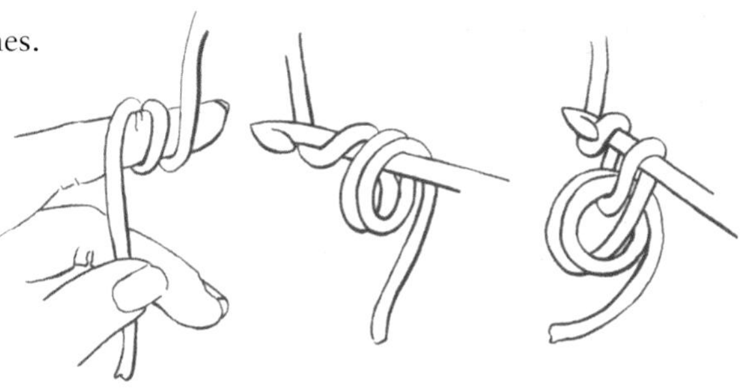

Figure 1 *Figure 2* *Figure 3*

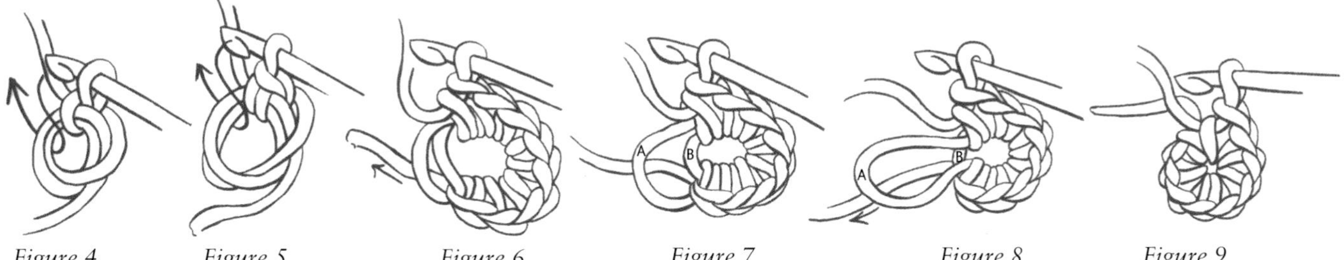

Figure 4 *Figure 5* *Figure 6* *Figure 7* *Figure 8* *Figure 9*

READING A PATTERN

Most projects are presented with written instructions called patterns. The pattern gives various sizes for the projects, the yarn, hooks, and notions you'll need, the all-critical gauge (see page 8), and the particular stitch patterns that are used.

Instructions are given for each piece of a project. They begin with the number of stitches to chain on and they end with fastening off a stitch. To save space, most instructions use standard abbreviations. For novices, it's not always easy to know what the abbreviations in a pattern mean. First, get comfortable with the basics, then crochet projects that use the "crocheter's shorthand."

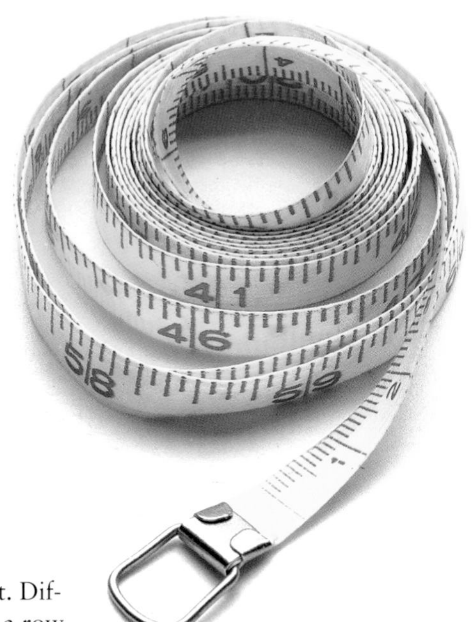

Before you begin to crochet, read through the instructions and make sure you understand how to do each part. Then read one sentence at a time. Each sentence represents one row or a series of rows that are worked the same way. Pay close attention to commas and semicolons because they usually indicate that something is changing in the next stitch or section. In some instructions, a series of stitches is repeated. The part to be repeated (called the pattern repeat) is usually set off with an asterisk (*) at either end.

Here are some common phrases in crochet patterns that will help you understand what to do.

Pattern Repeat

A pattern repeat refers to the number of stitches and rows that form a design in a unit. Different sizes of the same pattern will have a different number of pattern repeats across a row. A pattern repeat can contain as few as two stitches or as many as the width of the garment.

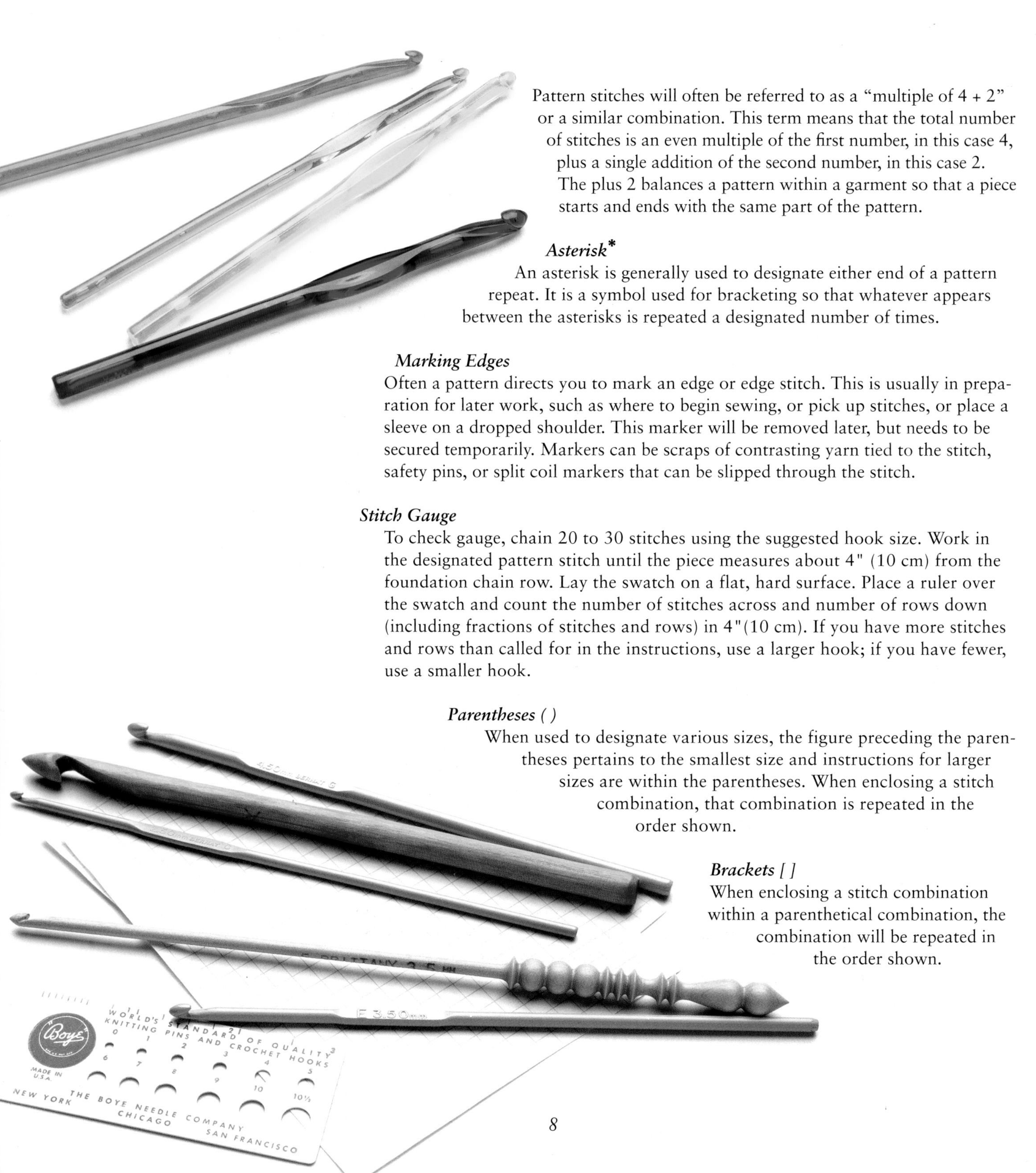

Pattern stitches will often be referred to as a "multiple of 4 + 2" or a similar combination. This term means that the total number of stitches is an even multiple of the first number, in this case 4, plus a single addition of the second number, in this case 2. The plus 2 balances a pattern within a garment so that a piece starts and ends with the same part of the pattern.

*Asterisk**

An asterisk is generally used to designate either end of a pattern repeat. It is a symbol used for bracketing so that whatever appears between the asterisks is repeated a designated number of times.

Marking Edges

Often a pattern directs you to mark an edge or edge stitch. This is usually in preparation for later work, such as where to begin sewing, or pick up stitches, or place a sleeve on a dropped shoulder. This marker will be removed later, but needs to be secured temporarily. Markers can be scraps of contrasting yarn tied to the stitch, safety pins, or split coil markers that can be slipped through the stitch.

Stitch Gauge

To check gauge, chain 20 to 30 stitches using the suggested hook size. Work in the designated pattern stitch until the piece measures about 4" (10 cm) from the foundation chain row. Lay the swatch on a flat, hard surface. Place a ruler over the swatch and count the number of stitches across and number of rows down (including fractions of stitches and rows) in 4"(10 cm). If you have more stitches and rows than called for in the instructions, use a larger hook; if you have fewer, use a smaller hook.

Parentheses ( )

When used to designate various sizes, the figure preceding the parentheses pertains to the smallest size and instructions for larger sizes are within the parentheses. When enclosing a stitch combination, that combination is repeated in the order shown.

Brackets [ ]

When enclosing a stitch combination within a parenthetical combination, the combination will be repeated in the order shown.

FINISHING TECHNIQUES

Weaving in Ends

Finishing Ends: At the end of the last row, don't make a turning chain. Cut the yarn leaving a 4" (10 cm) tail for weaving in. Insert the tail through the last stitch on hook and pull to tighten and secure (Figure 1).

In Seam Allowances: When working in rows, weave the yarn ends into the seam allowances whenever possible. If there isn't a seam allowance, weave the ends into the wrong side of work catching the back side of the crochet stitch (Figure 2).

In Rounds: When working in rounds, weave the ends vertically into the back of the work (Figure 3).

Figure 1

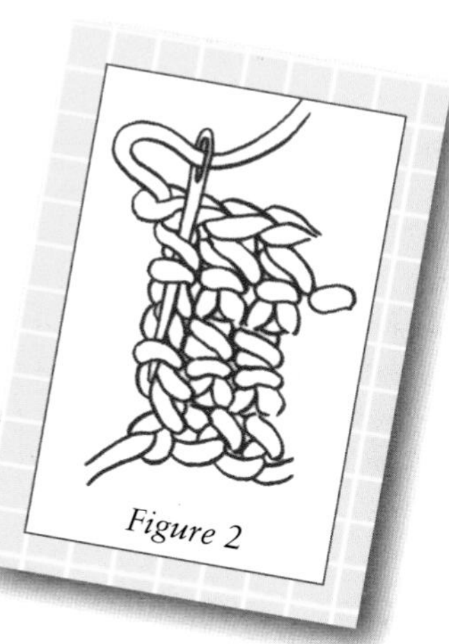
Figure 2

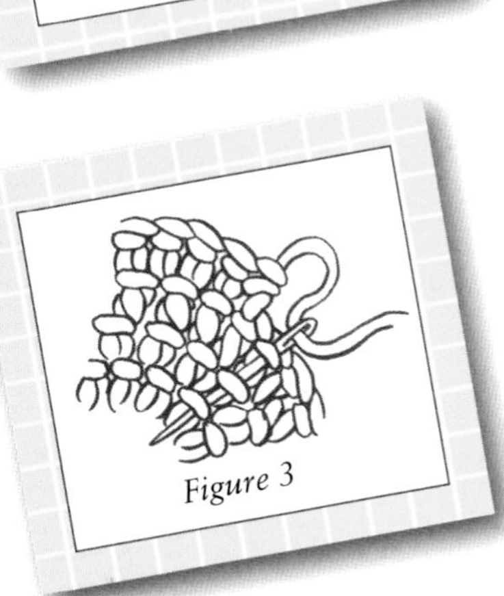
Figure 3

SEAMING

Single Crochet Method:

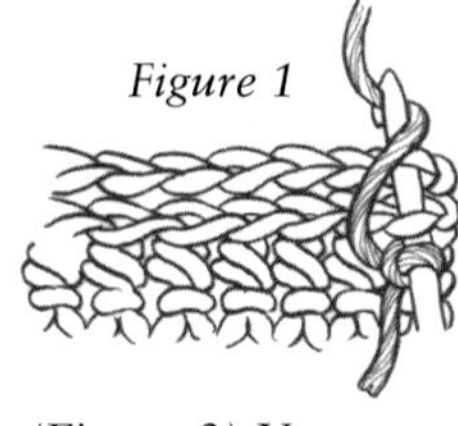
Figure 1

(Figure 1) Place the two pieces to be joined, right sides together, making sure the stitches or rows match exactly. With a slipknot on hook, insert the hook through the front loop of the first stitch of the first piece and the back loop of the first stitch of the second piece.

(Figure 2) Yarn over and draw a loop through both loops. Yarn over and draw a loop through the two loops on the hook—one single crochet made. Insert the hook into the next two stitches and single crochet in these two loops. Continue in this manner across row to the end of the seam. Fasten off and weave in ends.

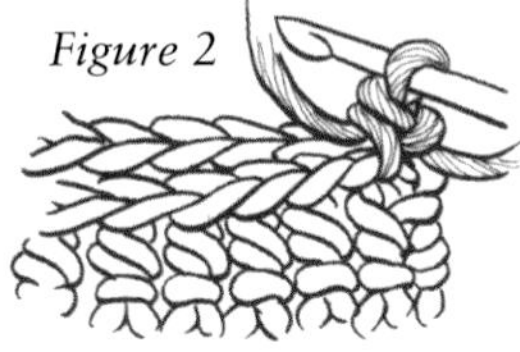
Figure 2

Slip-Stitch Method:

(Figure) Work as for first step above. Yarn over and draw yarn through both stitches and through loop on hook to complete the stitch. Continue in this manner across row to the end of the seam. Fasten off and weave in ends.

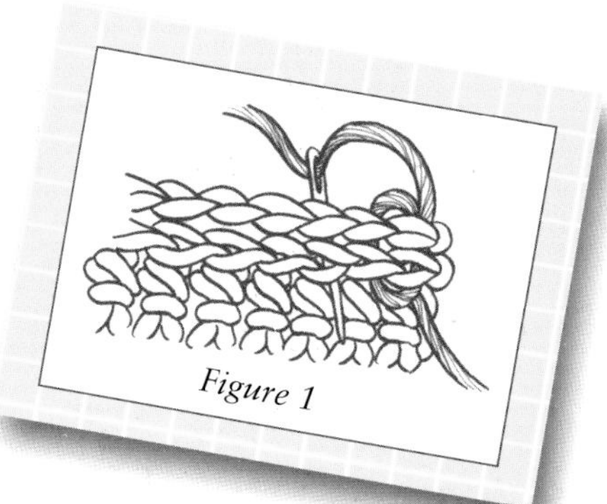
Figure 1

Backstitch:

A backstitch makes a very strong seam that doesn't stretch.

(Figure 1) Place the two pieces to be joined, right sides together, making sure the stitches or rows match exactly.

Starting from the right, insert the needle from front to back in the first stitch, and then from back to front in the next stitch to the left. Pass the needle from front to back again at the point where you began, and bring it out from back to front two stitches to the left.

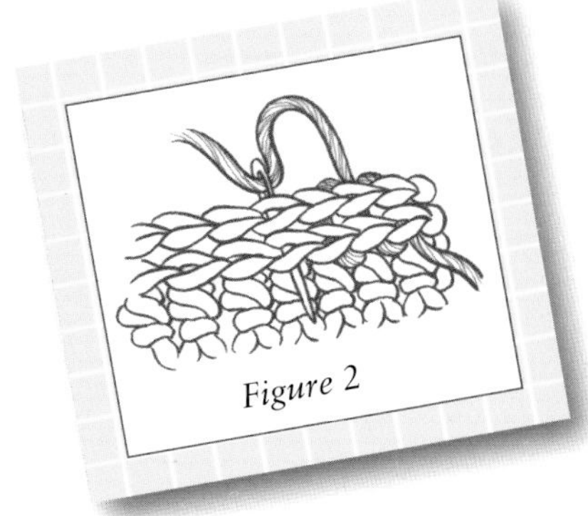
Figure 2

(Figure 2) Make subsequent stitches from front to back at the end of the preceding stitch, and from back to front two stitches to the left. Work to the end of the seam, fasten off, and weave in ends.

Whipstitch:

Place the two pieces to be joined, right sides together, making sure the stitches or rows match exactly. Starting from the right, insert the needle from back to front in the first stitch. Make subsequent stitches by bringing the needle over the top of the work and inserting it from back to front in the next stitch to the left. Work to the end of the seam, fasten off, and weave in ends.

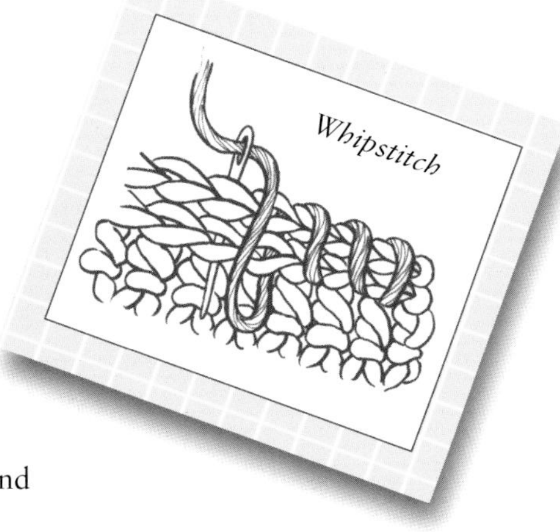
Whipstitch

Side Seam:

With right sides facing you, place the two pieces to be seamed together, edge to edge. Secure the yarn at the beginning of the first row on one piece, then pass the needle through the post of this row. Pass the needle through the corresponding post (see Working Stitches, page 3) on the second piece. Pass the needle through the post of the next row on the first piece. Work to the end of the seam, fasten off, and weave in ends.

Side Seam

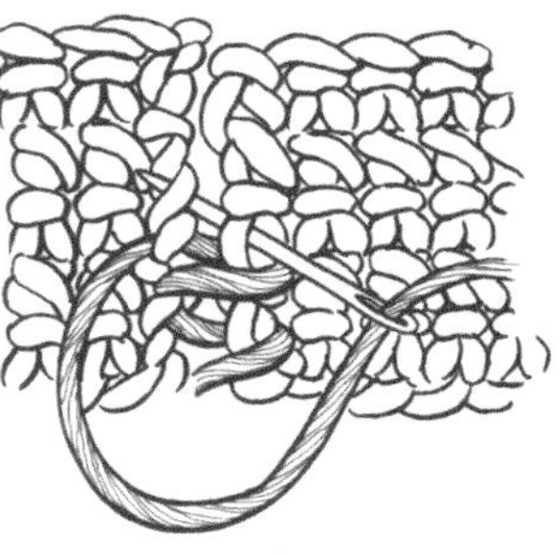

Shoulder Seam:

Place the two pieces to be joined, right sides together, making sure the stitches match exactly. Working from the armhole toward the neck, take a small stitch through the center of the first stitch on one piece, then take a small stitch through the center of the first stitch on the other piece. Continue in this manner, matching the seam stitch for stitch. Fasten off and weave in ends.

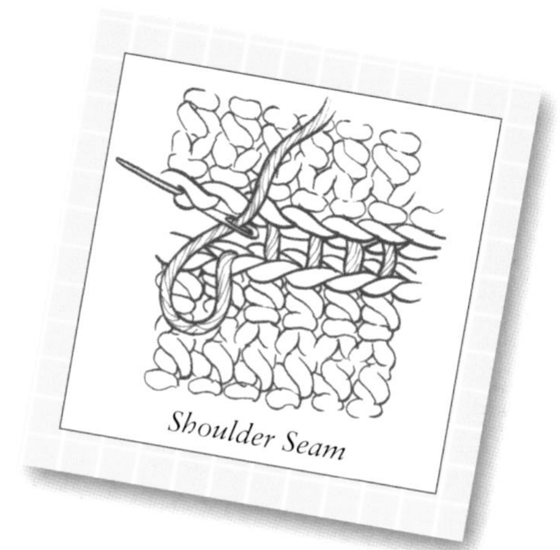

Shoulder Seam

BLOCKING

There's one more step that adds that finishing touch to a crocheted piece—blocking. This process helps eliminate any unevenness from your crocheting, smooths the seams, and sets the drape. There are two ways of blocking, either by steam or wetting down the piece. It's preferable to block individual pieces before sewing them together as it can make the sewing process easier. But you can also block the whole piece once your project is sewn together.

You'll need a few things to block your garment—a surface you can stick pins into, rustproof pins, a measuring device, and the finished dimensions of the piece. The surface can be as simple as a large towel spread out on a padded carpet or the top of your bed. The easiest pins to use are T-pins or pins with glass heads. The measuring device can be a yardstick or a nonstretching tape measure. Use the pattern schematic to check the size you're pinning your garment out to.

You can use your steam iron for steam blocking. Hold it a short distance above the crocheted piece to allow the steam to penetrate the fibers. Once you've steamed the full surface, let it dry before removing the pins.

Wet blocking uses more moisture than steam-blocking and can be used to stretch and enlarge a crocheted piece. Once you've pinned out the piece, use a spray-mist bottle with a fine, even mist. Gently pat the moisture into the piece. Again, let it dry before you remove the pins. During the blocking process, steam or wet, remember not to flatten any raised stitches.

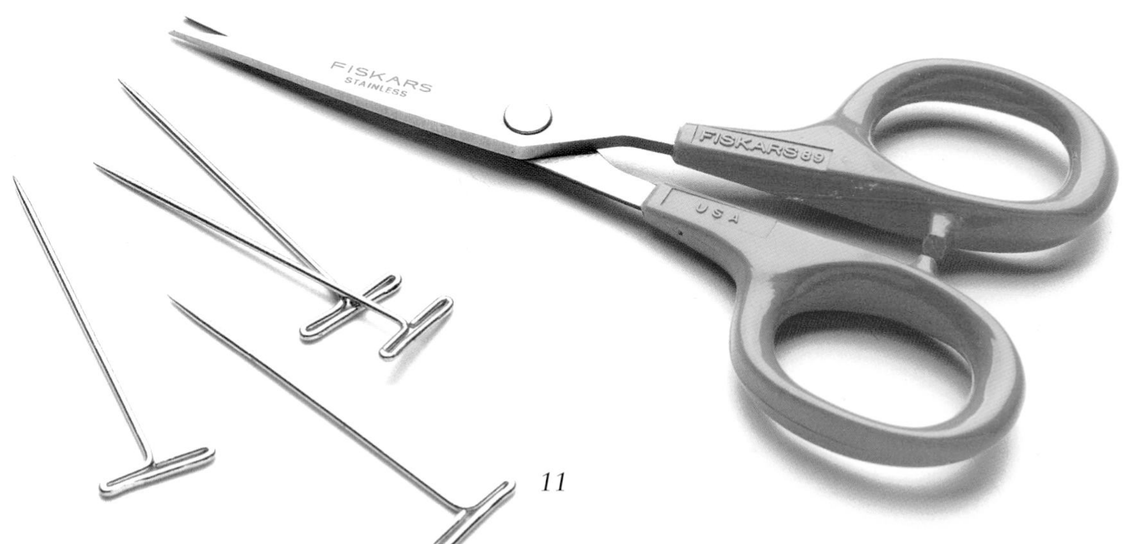

HOW HIP IS YOUR FIT?

One advantage of crocheting your own sweater is your ability to make it exactly the size and fit that you want. With some careful measuring and simple math, alterations to a pattern can be crocheted as you go along or, better yet, planned for before you even start. Still, many new crocheters are put off by taking measurements and choosing sizes, and they find it a daunting and mystifying task instead of an empowering opportunity.

The first step is to determine which size of pattern instructions to follow. Simply measure an existing garment that fits the way you want your sweater to fit. Lay the garment out on a flat surface and measure the key points—width, length, and sleeve length. Patterns generally include schematic drawings with all key measurements spelled out. Compare these measurements to your garment and choose a corresponding size. Keep in mind, however, that differences in yarn weight and gauge can affect fit. For instance, a sweater crocheted with lightweight yarn usually has more ability to drape than a bulky one where extra fabric bunches up.

Next, take into consideration how the garment is to be worn. Do you want it to fit next to your body or over layers of clothes? Is it an outdoor garment for winter or a summer top? A sweater coat, even if it is slim-fitting, requires more ease than a tank top. Note any changes you make to a pattern, such as "make sleeves two inches shorter." Generally speaking, length measurement changes are easier to adjust than width changes. Therefore, choose the pattern size option closest to the desired width and work from there to personalize the fit.

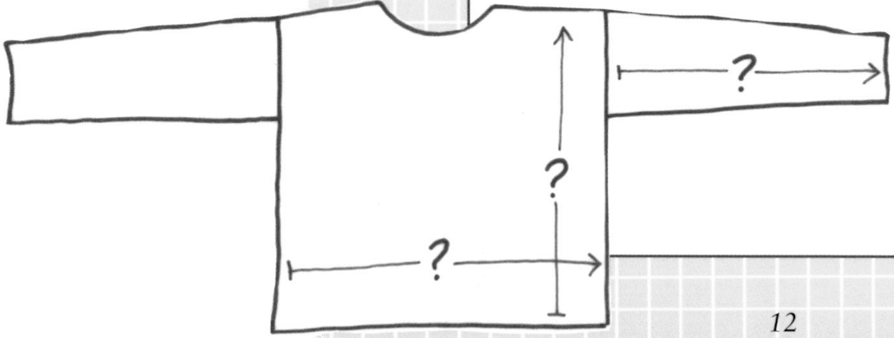

Garments are often described as close-fitting, standard-fitting, loose-fitting or oversized. These terms refer to the size of the garment in comparison to body measurements, particularly bust/chest circumference. For this reason, you need to measure the bust or chest at the fullest part. A close-fitting garment is the same measurement, or sometimes an inch or two smaller. A standard-fitting garment is about two or three inches larger than the body measurement, or it contains two to three inches of ease. A loose-fitting garment contains about five inches of ease, and an oversized garment is at least six inches larger than the body. Remember that choosing a size by following these guidelines produces a garment sized as the pattern designer intended. However, there is no law that says a crocheter must follow these guidelines, and this is where you have the opportunity to individualize the look and fit of a pattern. Just make sure that the lines of the garment lend themselves to your alternative interpretation. For instance: Dropped shoulders generally look better in a garment that is at least somewhat oversized, while set-in sleeves are pretty versatile and can withstand dramatic changes in fit interpretation. Very full sleeves need to be tapered to keep proportion with a fitted body. If you feel that everything needs changing, you should choose a different pattern.

Fashions change often, but a good sweater design can be timeless. A dated photograph does not necessarily mean a dated design. Too often people cannot see beyond an existing presentation, even as far as changing the color! Sometimes a classic pattern just needs a change in fit to renew it. Would that cardigan be perfect if it were several inches shorter? What if it was body-skimming instead of standard-fitting?

A basic garment can easily go from stodgy to hip with minor alterations. Learning to look critically at a design in order to personalize it is a skill worth developing. *Hip to Crochet* includes garments in multiple sizes to accommodate both different shapes and preferences in fit. In choosing patterns to crochet, look at basic shapes and then think about how to change them to express the wearer's personality.

MY FIRST
SCARF

If you need a "perfect" first project, this is it. The scarf uses only one stitch, and the stripes are easy to measure. Practice changing color and making even edges as you crochet the stripes. Depending on your mood or your wardrobe, use as few or as many colors as you want. Heck, make a scarf for every day of the week.

SPECIFICATIONS

SIZE	YARN	HOOK	NOTIONS	GAUGE
9" (23 cm) wide × 70" (178 cm) long, excluding fringe.	Double-knitting weight yarn, about 800 yd (732 m). ***We used:*** Jo Sharp DK Wool distributed by Knitting Fever (100% wool; 107 yd [98 m]/50 g): 2 balls #004 Dijon (A), 1 skein each #803 lichen (B), #318 forest (C), #804 embers (D), #325 mulberry (E), #307 wine (F), #003 tangerine (G).	Size G/6 (4.5 mm). Adjust hook size if necessary to obtain the correct gauge.	Cardboard (4 × 6") [10 × 15 cm] for wrapping fringe; tapestry needle.	18 stitches and 11 rows = 4" (10 cm) in half double crochet with size G/6 (4.5 mm) hook.

ABBREVIATIONS

ch(s)—chain(s)
hdc—half double crochet
lp(s)—loop(s)
rep—repeat
st(s)—stitch(es)

Review Basics, page 2
Chain stitch
Half double crochet
Reading a pattern
Slipknot
Weaving in ends

SCARF

With hook and color A, loosely ch 43 sts.
Row 1: Starting in third ch from hook, work 40 hdc—41 sts, counting ch-2 as first st. Turn.
Row 2: Ch 2 (counts as 1 hdc), work 40 hdc across row—41 hdc. Turn.
Rep Row 2 for pattern, working 4 rows per color in sequence, beginning with A through G, and rep the entire color sequence a total of 8 times—28 rows total. Work 4 more rows in color A. Fasten off as follows: Cut yarn leaving 4" (10 cm) tail, insert tail through last st on hook and pull to tighten and secure.

FINISHING

Thread loose ends on tapestry needle and weave along side edges or wrong side of work to secure. Cut 24 twelve-inch strands of each color, using cardboard as measuring guide to make the fringe. Following the color sequence of striping and using 4 strands per fringe, attach fringe to every other stitch on both ends of the scarf (see page 17). Trim fringe ends to even length.

DESIGNING YOUR OWN SCARF

A scarf is one of the easiest pieces to design, and these tips will ensure a professional-looking result. First, figure out the size you want the scarf to be. Then figure out how many stitches to chain. Multiply the gauge (see Basics, page 8), using the stitch you select for the scarf by the desired finished width. For example, if your gauge is 4 stitches to the inch and the scarf is to be 9" (23 cm) wide (average width is 8–12" [20.5–30.5 cm]), you will chain 36 stitches plus a turning chain. The average length of a scarf is 48–60" [122–152.5 cm]).

But what about choosing a stitch pattern? Crocheted fabric can become very dense, especially a scarf done entirely in single crochet. If single crochet is your chosen stitch, be sure the hook is large enough to make a flexible fabric. In general, a long stitch like double crochet, or an open stitch like lace is best suited for a scarf.

Joining motifs together, such as for the Kaleidoscope Scarf on page 44, presents other options. Remember that you may have to adjust your stitch count from the gauge measurement count to accommodate the number of stitches for your pattern repeat.

Make your gauge swatch in the stitch you select for the scarf and remember that it is generally desirable that a scarf fabric have more drape than a sweater. A scarf is therefore usually worked with a hook one or two sizes larger than one would use for a sweater of the same yarn.

The amount of yarn required for the scarf will vary with the width and length, but you can estimate using about 30% of the yarn needed for an average sweater. In sportweight yarn, estimate using about 500 yd (461 m), in worsted-weight yarn 450 yd (488 m), and in bulky yarn 350 yd (379 m). However, some stitch patterns use more yarn than others. To make sure you have enough yarn, check the number of square inches completed with the first full skein in the chosen stitch pattern and gauge. Then divide that number of square inches into the total square inches in your scarf. For example, if one skein makes 9" in width by 20" in length (23 × 51 cm), that equals 180 square inches. If your finished scarf is to be 9" by 60" (23 × 152.5 cm), it will have 540 square inches, not including fringe. Divide the 180 square inches made by the first skein into the 540 square inches needed to complete the scarf, and the result is 3. You will therefore need at least 3 skeins to complete the scarf, plus extra yarn for the fringe.

CHANGING COLORS

The technique for changing colors or adding new yarn is easy, especially when you're crocheting dense patterns. Cut the end of the color you are discontinuing to about 6" (15 cm). Begin working the new color in the next stitch, holding both the cut end and the new end taut in your left hand and laying both ends over the top of the stitches to be worked. Continue working the pattern as established, but for several stitches the ends will lie on top of the work and you will crochet over them with the new yarn as you work into each stitch (Figure). Once the new yarn is secure, release the ends, but work a few more stitches over them. Trim ends and continue working with the new yarn. **Note:** If the yarns are bulky, work the new end in for a few stitches more than the old end just to grade the bulk. This method of working in ends as you go keeps your edges secure and allows you to work neatly and eliminate time-consuming finishing at the end of the project.

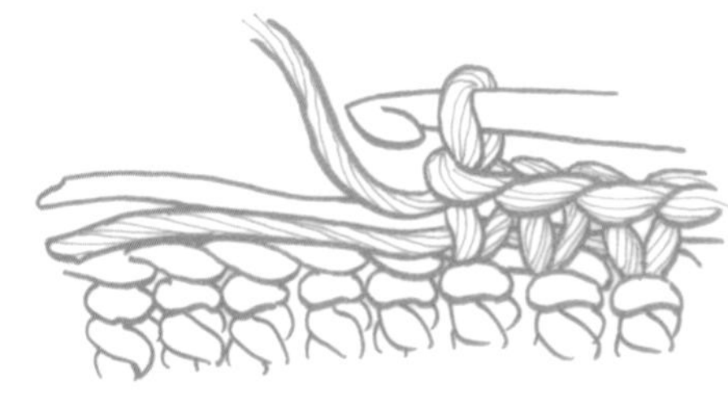

Figure

If you're working a multicolored pattern and carrying colors, you can use this same method *but* don't cut the yarn, simply carry it along and bring it into use as the pattern indicates.

When you change colors in an open pattern, or start a new thread, you may not be able to conceal ends as easily. In this case, cut the thread being discontinued and leave a tail of about 6" (15 cm). Pick up the new thread and begin working with it holding both ends taut until it is secure, but instead of working over both ends, leave them at the edge of the work to be secured later. If the edge of the work goes into a seam allowance, secure the ends in the seam. In the case of a scarf or shawl where there are no seams, work the tails back into the fabric following pattern stitches to conceal the ends as much as possible (see Basics, page 9).

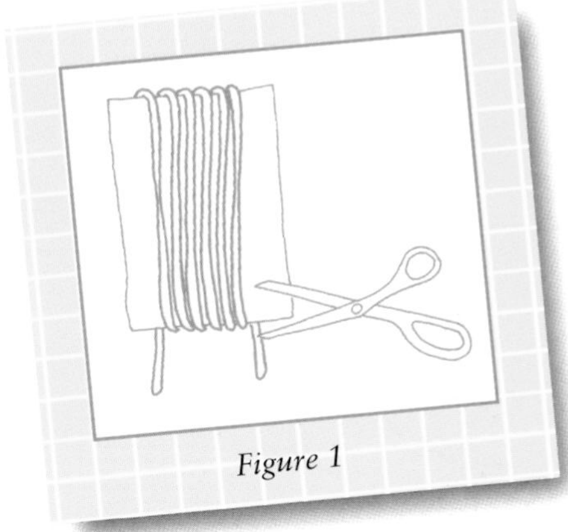

Figure 1

BASIC FRINGE

To cut even lengths of fringe, you will need a stiff cardboard about 1" (2.5 cm) longer than the finished length of the fringe. Starting and ending at the bottom edge, wrap the yarn around the cardboard once for each strand desired. Cut across the bottom edge (Figure 1). Fold the fringe strands in half, bring the crochet hook through the edge of crochet, and pull folded fringe partway through work. Insert hook through the loop that is formed (Figure 2) and pull the ends of the fringe through the loop and down to straighten and tighten.

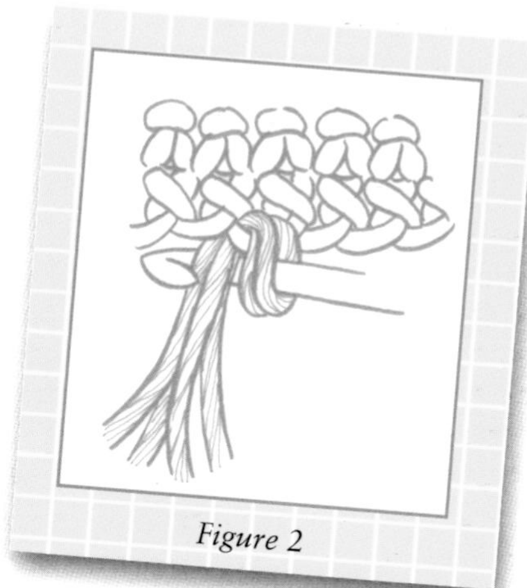

Figure 2

ONE-OF-A-KIND

HATS

You'll never have to make the same hat twice. Use this one as the basis for others. Change textures and colors, use stripes, add ear flaps, cuff it or embellish it. You choose.

S P E C I F I C A T I O N S

SIZE

23" (58.5 cm) circumference, 9" (23 cm) long excluding peak, measured straight down from top (unfolded).

YARN

Sportweight yarn, about 250 yd (229 m). ***We used:*** Rowan Cotton Glace (100% cotton; 125 yd [115 m]/50 g): 2 balls #741 poppy.

HOOK

Size F/5 (4 mm). Adjust hook size if necessary to obtain correct gauge.

NOTIONS

Tapestry needle.

GAUGE

19 stitches and 11.5 rows = 4" (10 cm) in half double crochet with size F/5 (4 mm) hook.

SOLID HAT

ABBREVIATIONS

beg—begin(s), beginning
ch—chain
hdc—half double crochet
inc—increase(s)
lp(s)—loop(s)
rep—repeat
rnd(s)—round(s)
sk—skip
sl st—slip stitch
st(s)—stitch(es)
yo—yarn over

Review Basics, page 2
Chain stitch
Decreasing
Half double crochet
Increasing
Reading a pattern
Slipknot
Weaving in ends
Working in rounds

HAT

With hook and yarn, ch 4 sts, join into a ring (see page 23) as follows: Insert hook into first ch made and join to lp on hook with sl st to form the ring.

Rnd 1: Ch 2 (counts as 1 hdc), work 6 hdc into the center of the ring. Join rnd with sl st to top of ch—7 hdc.

Rnd 2: Ch 2 (counts as 1 hdc), sk first hdc, work 1 hdc in each hdc to end of rnd. Join rnd with sl st to top of ch—7 hdc.

Rnd 3: Ch 2 (counts as 1 hdc), sk first hdc, *work 1 hdc in next hdc, work 2 hdc in next hdc (inc made)*; rep from * to * to last st, work 1 hdc. Join rnd with sl st to top of ch—10 hdc.

Rnd 4: Ch 2 (counts as 1 hdc), sk first hdc, *work 2 hdc in each hdc to end of rnd. Join rnd with sl st to top of ch—19 hdc.

Rnd 5: Ch 2 (counts as 1 hdc), sk first hdc, *work 1 hdc in next hdc, work 2 hdc in next hdc*; rep from * to * to end of rnd. Join rnd with sl st to top of ch—28 hdc.
Rnd 6: Ch 2 (counts as 1 hdc), sk first hdc *work 1 hdc in each of next 2 hdc, work 2 hdc in next hdc*; rep from * to * to end of rnd. Join rnd with sl st to top of ch—37 hdc.
Rnd 7: Ch 2 (counts as 1 hdc) sk first hdc, *work 1 hdc in each of next 3 hdc, work 2 hdc in next hdc*; rep from * to * to end of rnd. Join rnd with sl st to top of ch—46 hdc.
Rnd 8: Ch 2 (counts as 1 hdc), sk first hdc, *work 1 hdc in each of next 4 hdc, work 2 hdc in next hdc*; rep from * to * to end of rnd. Join rnd with sl st to top of ch—55 hdc.
Rnd 9: Ch 2 (counts as 1 hdc), sk first hdc, *work 1 hdc in each of next 5 hdc, work 2 hdc in next hdc*; rep from * to * to end of rnd. Join rnd with sl st to top of ch—64 hdc.
Rnd 10: Ch 2 (counts as 1 hdc), sk first hdc, *work 1 hdc in each of next 6 hdc, work 2 hdc in next hdc*; rep from * to * to end of rnd. Join rnd with sl st to top of ch—73 hdc.
Rnd 11: Ch 2 (counts as 1 hdc), skip first hdc, *work 1 hdc in each of next 7 hdc, work 2 hdc in next hdc*; rep from * to * to end of rnd. Join rnd with sl st to top of ch—82 hdc.
Rnd 12: Ch 2 (counts as 1 hdc), sk first hdc, *work 1 hdc in each of next 8 hdc, work 2 hdc in next hdc*; rep from * to * to end of rnd. Join rnd with sl st to top of ch—91 hdc.
Rnd 13: Ch 2 (counts as 1 hdc), sk first hdc, *work 1 hdc in each of next 9 hdc, work 2 hdc in next hdc*; rep from * to * to end of rnd. Join rnd with sl st to top of ch—100 hdc.
Rnd 14: Ch 2 (counts as 1 hdc), sk first hdc, *work 1 hdc in each of next 10 hdc, work 2 hdc in next hdc*; rep from * to * to end of rnd. Join rnd with sl st to top of ch—109 hdc.
Work even in hdc on 109 sts until piece measures a total length of 9½" (24 cm) from beg ch. Fasten off as follows: Cut yarn leaving 4" (10 cm) tail, insert tail through last lp on hook and pull to tighten and secure.

Solid Hat

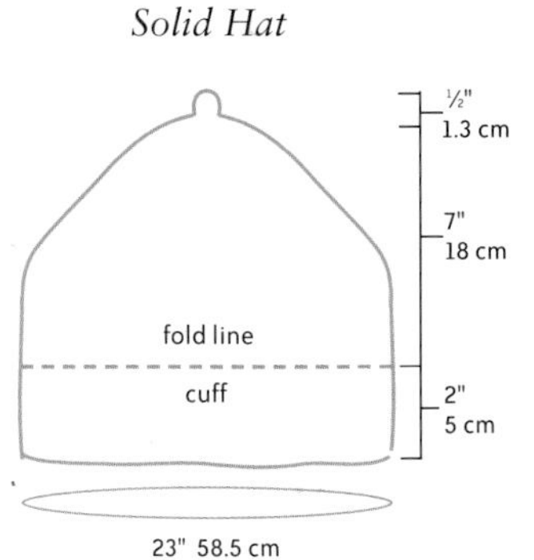

FINISHING

Thread loose yarn ends on tapestry needle and weave through sts on wrong side of work. Turn up 2" (5 cm) around bottom edge for cuff.

PERFECT POM-POMS

1. Cut two cardboard circles ½" (1.3 cm) larger in diameter than the desired finished size. Cut a ¾" (2-cm) hole in the center of each circle. Cut away a small wedge of each circle to make it easier to wrap the yarn. Place a tie strand of yarn between the circles and hold them together, with both openings together. Wrap yarn around the circles the desired number of times (the more wraps, the thicker the pom-pom).

2. Insert scissors between circles and carefully cut around the outer edge to release the yarn. Knot the tie strand tightly around the group of yarn. Gently ease the cardboard from the pom-pom.

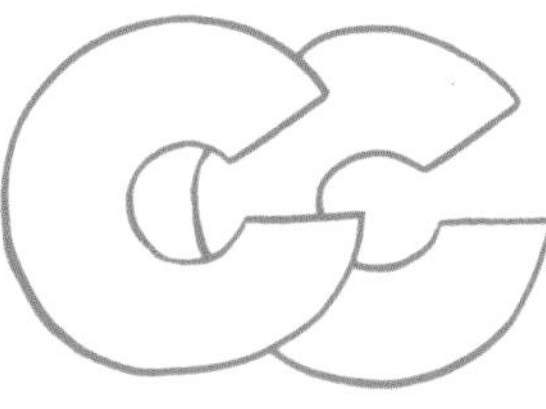

Step 1

SPECIFICATIONS

SIZE

22" (56 cm) circumference, 7½" (19 cm) long, excluding peak, measured straight down from top.

YARN

Double-knitting weight yarn, about 220 yd (201 m) total. ***We used:*** Jo Sharp DK Wool distributed by Knitting Fever (100% wool; 107 yd [98 m]/50 g); 2 balls #803 lichen (A), 1 skein each #307 wine (B), #318 forest (C), #004 Dijon (D), #325 mulberry (E).

HOOK

Size G/6 (4.5 mm). Adjust hook size if necessary to obtain the correct gauge.

NOTIONS

Tapestry needle.

GAUGE

18 stitches and 12 rows = 4" (10 cm) in half double crochet with size G/6 (4.5 mm) hook.

STRIPED HAT

HAT

With hook and color A, work same as for Solid Hat through Rnd 13—100 hdc. Working even on 100 sts, continue in color A for 3 more rnds. ***Stripe Pattern:*** Continue working in hdc, work 1 rnd each in color B, C, D, E, D, C, B, and then 3 more rnds in color A. Fasten off as follows: Cut yarn leaving 4" (10 cm) tail, insert tail through last lp on hook and pull to tighten and secure.

FINISHING

Thread loose yarn ends on tapestry needle and weave through sts on wrong side of work. Steam hat lightly to block.

Striped Hat

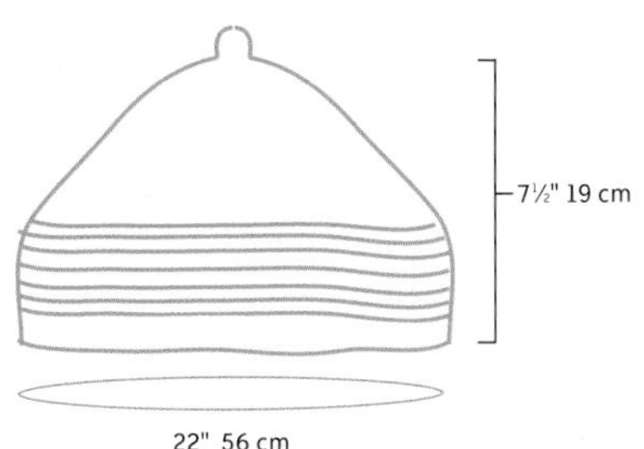

3. Cut two cardboard circles ½" (1.3 cm) smaller than the first two (the diameter of the desired finished size). Poke a pinpoint hole in the center of each circle. Sandwich the pom-pom between these two circles and insert a long tapestry needle through the hole in one circle, through the center of the pom-pom and out through the hole in the other circle. This will hold the pom-pom in place as you trim around the edges of the circles to even out the pom-pom.

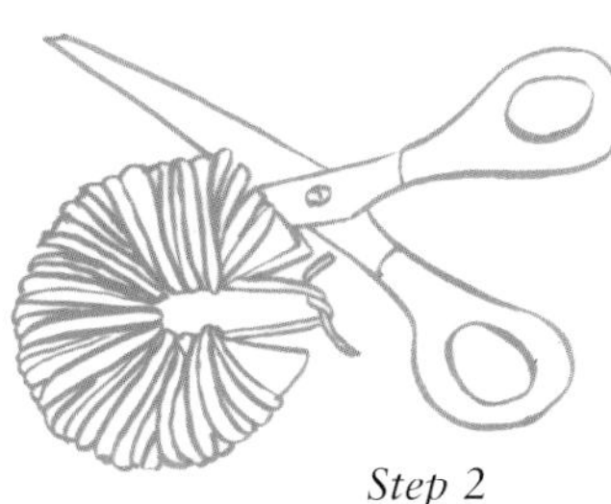

Step 2

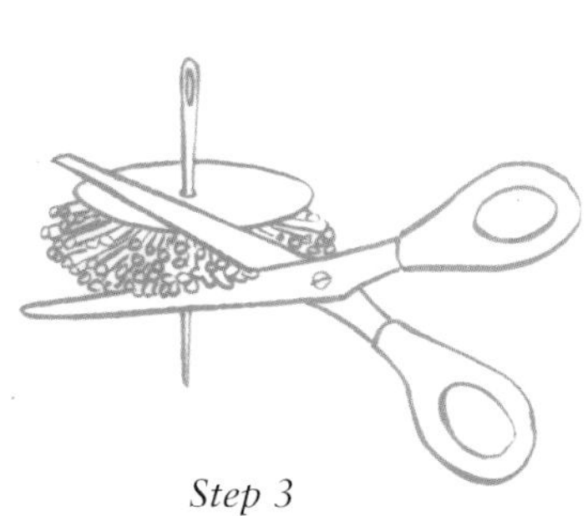

Step 3

SPECIFICATIONS

SIZE

22" (56 cm) circumference, 7½" (19 cm) long, excluding peak, measured straight down from top.

YARN

Double-knitting weight yarn, about 240 yd (220 m) total. ***We used:*** Jo Sharp Wool distributed by Knitting Fever (100% wool; 107 yd [98 m]/ 50 g); 2 balls # 003 tangerine (A), 1 ball each #803 lichen (B), #004 Dijon (C), #307 wine (D), #804 embers (E).

HOOK

Size G/6 (4.5 mm). Adjust hook size if necessary to obtain the correct gauge.

NOTIONS

Cardboard circles, about 3" (7.5 cm) in diameter for making pom-poms; tapestry needle.

GAUGE

18 stitches and 12 rows = 4" (10 cm) in half double crochet with size G/6 (4.5mm) hook.

Ear-Flap Hat

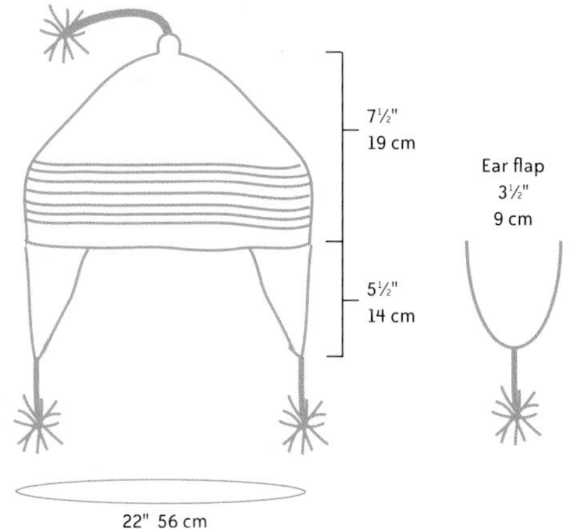

EAR-FLAP HAT

HAT

Work the same as for Striped Hat. When finished, add ***Ear Flaps:*** Insert hook into the 13th st to the left of where hat is fastened off (center back) and attach color A. Ch 2 (counts as 1 hdc), work 1 hdc in each of next 15 hdc—16 hdc total. Working back and forth in rows, work 2 rows even.

Decrease Row: Ch 2, work a one-stitch decrease as follows: yo, insert hook into next st, yo and pull up a lp (3 lps on hook), yo and insert hook into next st, yo and pull up a lp (5 lps on hook), yo, and pull through all 5 lps at once, work even across row to last 3 sts, decrease one st same as before, end row with 1 hdc.

Next row: Work 1 row even. Rep last 2 rows decreasing 2 sts every other row until 4 sts remain. Fasten off. Insert hook into 28th st to the right of center back, join yarn and ch 2. Work 1 hdc in each of next 15 hdc—16 hdc total. Continue the same as for first ear flap. Fasten off as follows: Cut yarn leaving 4" (10 cm) tail, insert tail through last lp on hook and pull to tighten and secure.

FINISHING

Thread loose yarn ends on tapestry needle and weave through sts on wrong side of work. *Edging stitch:* With hook and color B, attach yarn at center back. With right side of work facing you, *work 1 sc in first hdc, ch 1, sk next hdc*; rep from * to * around to center of first ear flap. Ch 15, work 1 sl st in each ch to form a cord (see page 39); resume edging pattern around hat base to other ear flap and rep ch 15 and sl st cord in center of second ear flap, resume edging pattern to center back, and join first and last sc sts with sl st at end of rnd. Attach color B to top of peak, and ch 8, work 1 sl st in each chain to form a short cord. Fasten off. *Pom-poms* (see page 20): Make three pompoms using all colors. Attach one each to end of both earflap chains, and the third pom-pom to the chain end on top of hat.

WORKING IN ROUNDS

Working in rounds allows you to create seamless crochet shapes. Rounds can begin from a small chain and increase outward, adding stitches to each round to enlarge the circle and create a flat shape, or working around to create a tube. In this last method, the first round of stitches is usually worked into each chain stitch, instead of into the center of the ring. Because the same side of the work is always facing you, there will be a different look to the front and back of the crocheted fabric.

There are two methods of joining stitches when you work in rounds—separate or spiral. When you work separate rounds (see Separate Method below), start each round with the number of chains to approximate the height of the stitch in that round (chain 1 for single crochet, chain 2 for half double crochet, chain 3 for double crochet (see Basics, page 4). Stitches are then worked to the end of the round, and the round is joined together by slip-stitching to the top of the starting chain. This method is preferred when there are stripes or obvious pattern lines to match up. However, the joining line does not always blend invisibly into the work.

Working in the spiral fashion (see Spiral Method below) creates a smooth fabric. It is necessary to mark the beginning of each round for ease in working; otherwise it can be confusing to determine where the next round begins. When you're working in spiral fashion, rounds are not joined but worked continuously with no visible joining line.

JOIN INTO A RING

Separate Method

1. Chain four stitches and join into a ring by inserting hook into first chain and join to loop on hook with a slip stitch to form the ring. Chain two stitches—these approximate the height of the half double crochet. (Figure 1)
2. Work six half double crochet into the center of the ring and join round with a slip stitch to the top of the chain.
3. Chain two stitches, skip the first half double crochet, *work one half double crochet in next half double crochet, work two half double crochet in next half double crochet (an increase is made)*; repeat from * to * to last stitch, work one half double crochet. Join round with slip stitch to top of chain. You now have ten half double crochet. (Figure 2)

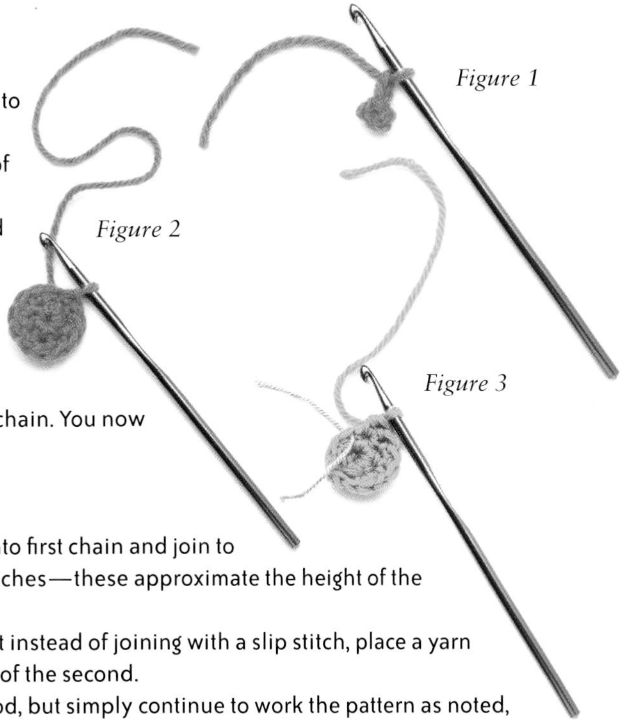

Figure 1

Figure 2

Figure 3

Spiral Method

1. Chain four stitches and join into a ring by inserting hook into first chain and join to loop on hook with a slip stitch to form the ring. Chain two stitches—these approximate the height of the half double crochet.
2. Work six half double crochet into the center of the ring, but instead of joining with a slip stitch, place a yarn marker to signal the end of the first round and the beginning of the second.
3. There is no need to chain stitches as in the separate method, but simply continue to work the pattern as noted, moving the yarn marker with every round. (Figure 3)

STRIPED

MITTENS

Not only are these mittens easy, you can make a pair to match any of the hats or scarves in this book and be completely accessorized. The short fringed edge adds flair.

S P E C I F I C A T I O N S

SIZE	YARN	HOOK	NOTIONS	GAUGE
9½" (24 cm) long, excluding fringe; 9½" (24 cm) circumference.	Double-knitting weight yarn, about 200 yd (185 m). ***We used:*** Jo Sharp DK Wool distributed by Knitting Fever (100% wool; 107 yd [98 m]/50 g): 2 balls #004 Dijon (MC), 1 skein each #325 mulberry (A), #318 forest (B), #803 lichen (C), #003 tangerine (D). **Note:** If you are making mittens to match the One-of-a-Kind Hats, there will be enough leftover yarn for the contrast stripes.	Size G/6 (4.5 mm). Adjust hook size if necessary to obtain the correct gauge.	Cardboard (4 × 6") [10 × 15 cm] for wrapping fringe; tapestry needle.	18 stitches and 11 rounds = 4" (10 cm) in half double crochet with size G/6 (4.5 mm) hook.

ABBREVIATIONS

beg —begin(s), beginning
ch(s)—chain(s)
dc—double crochet
hdc—half double crochet
lp(s)—loop(s)
MC—main color
rep—repeat
rnd(s)—round(s)
sc—single crochet
sl st—slip st
st(s)—stitch(es)

Review Basics, page 2:
Chain stitch
Half double crochet
Reading a pattern
Seaming
Slip stitch
Weaving in ends
Working in rounds

RIGHT MITTEN

Thumb: (Worked from tip to hand)

With hook and MC, ch 4 sts. Join into a ring (see page 23) as follows: Insert hook into first ch and join to lp on hook with sl st to form ring.

Rnd 1: Ch 2 (counts as 1 hdc), work 7 hdc into ring, join rnd with sl st to top of ch—8 hdc.

Rnd 2: Ch 2 (for height only, does not count as hdc), work 1 hdc in first st, work 2 hdc in next st, *work 1 hdc in next st, work 2 hdc in next st*; rep from * to * to end of rnd, join rnd with sl st to top of ch—12 hdc.

Rnd 3: Ch 2 (does not count as hdc), work 1 hdc in each st to end of rnd, join rnd with sl st to top of ch—12 hdc.
Rep Rnd 3 until thumb measures 3" (7.5 cm) long. Fasten off as follows: Cut yarn leaving 4" (10 cm) tail, insert tail through lp on hook and pull to tighten.

HAND

(Worked from finger tips to wrist)
With hook and MC, ch 4 sts. Join with sl st to form a ring.
Rnd 1: Ch 2 (counts as 1 hdc), work 7 hdc into ring, join rnd with sl st to top of ch—8 hdc.
Rnd 2: Ch 2 (does not count as 1 hdc), work 1 hdc in first hdc, work 2 hdc in next hdc, *work 1 hdc in next hdc, work 2 hdc in next hdc*; rep from * to * to end of rnd, join rnd with sl st to top of ch—12 hdc.
Rnd 3: Ch 2 (does not count as 1 hdc), work 1 hdc in each of first 2 hdc, work 2 hdc in next hdc, *work 1 hdc in each of next 2 hdc, work 2 hdc in next hdc*; rep from * to * to end of rnd, join rnd with sl st to top of ch—16 hdc.
Rnd 4: Ch 2 (does not count as 1 hdc), work 1 hdc in each of first 3 hdc, work 2 hdc in next hdc, *work 1 hdc in each of next 3 hdc, work 2 hdc in next hdc*; rep from * to * to end of rnd, join rnd with sl st to top of ch—20 hdc.

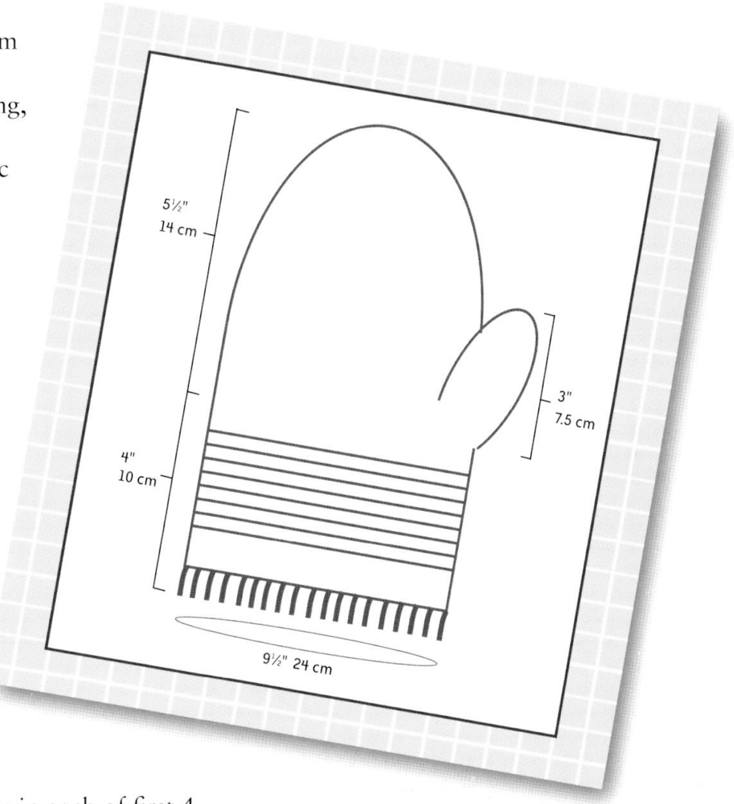

Rnd 5: Ch 2 (does not count as 1 hdc), work 1 hdc in first hdc, work 1 hdc in each hdc to end of rnd, join rnd with sl st to top of ch.
Rnd 6: Ch 2 (does not count as 1 hdc), work 1 hdc in each of first 4 hdc, work 2 hdc in next hdc, *work 1 hdc in each of next 4 hdc, work 2 hdc in next hdc*; rep from * to * to end of rnd, join rnd with sl st to top of ch—24 hdc.
Rnd 7: Rep Rnd 5.
Rnd 8: Ch 2 (does not count as 1 hdc), work 1 hdc in each of first 5 hdc, work 2 hdc in next hdc, *work 1 hdc in each of next 5 hdc, work 2 hdc in next hdc*; rep from * to * to end of rnd, join rnd with sl st to top of ch—28 hdc.
Rnd 9: Rep Rnd 5.
Rnd 10: Ch 2 (does not count as 1 hdc), work 1 hdc in each of first 6 hdc, work 2 hdc in next hdc, *work 1 hdc in each of next 6 hdc, work 2 hdc in next hdc*; rep from * to * to end of rnd, join rnd with sl st to top of ch—32 hdc.
Rnd 11: Rep Rnd 5.
Rnd 12: Ch 2 (does not count as 1 hdc), work 1 hdc in each of first 7 hdc, work 2 hdc in next hdc, *work 1 hdc in each of next 7 hdc, work 2 hdc in next hdc*; rep

from * to * to end of rnd, join rnd with sl st to top of ch—36 hdc.

Work even in rnds as established on 36 hdc to a total length of 5½" (14 cm).

Join thumb: On next rnd, ch 2 (does not count as st), work 1 hdc in first hdc, work 1 hdc in each of 9 hdc sts of thumb, sk next 3 hdc sts on hand, work 1 hdc in each of next 32 hdc sts of hand, join rnd to top of ch—42 hdc.

Note: The 3 sts each on hand and thumb that were not worked will be stitched together later.

Next Rnd: In MC, ch 2 (does not count as st), work sc in each of 42 hdc to end of rnd, join rnd to top of ch with sl st.

Stripe Pattern: (See Changing Colors, page 17); Ch 1 (does not count as st), sc 1 rnd each in colors A, B, C, D, C, B, A—7 rnds total.

Work 3 more rnds in MC. Fasten off.

LEFT MITTEN

Work same as Right Mitten to thumb joining.

Join Thumb: Ch 1 (does not count as st), work 1 hdc in each of first 17 hdc of next rnd, work 1 hdc in each of 9 thumb sts, sk next 3 sts on hand, work 1 hdc in each of next 16 hdc on hand, join rnd to top of ch with sl st—42 hdc.

Continue mitten same as for Right Mitten.

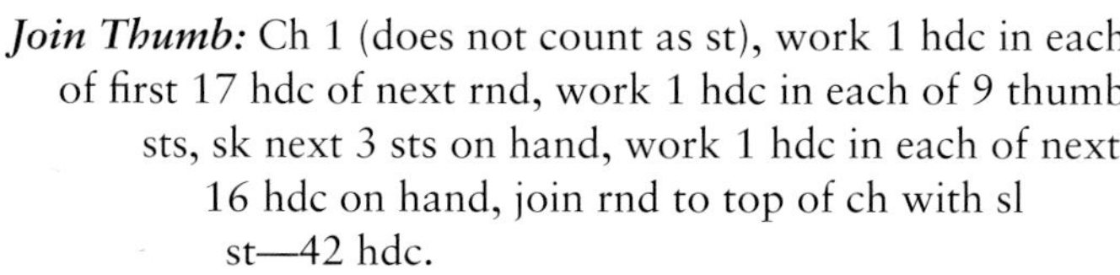

■ **FINISHING**

Weave in loose ends. Turn mitten inside out and sew together the open edges of thumb and hand—the 3 sts on each not previously joined. Edge Fringe (see Basic Fringe, page 17): Using cardboard as a guide, cut sixteen 12-inch (30.5-cm) pieces of each color by wrapping yarn around lengthwise and cutting at one end. Cut each piece in half again. Using a crochet hook, work two strands of yarn through each stitch around the lower mitten edge, creating an appealing color sequence.

STRIPES

Stripes are an easy way to add multiple colors to your work. They can be as narrow or as bold as you desire and you can use many colors in one project. Several shades of one hue give a subtle, almost dimensional effect, while contrasting colors create a vibrant effect. Color placement can influence the perception of a hue as can the width of a stripe.

An easy and interesting way to vary the width of a crocheted stripe is to change the stitch varying from single crochet to treble crochet. This not only adds texture to the fabric, but also adds interest to the stripes.

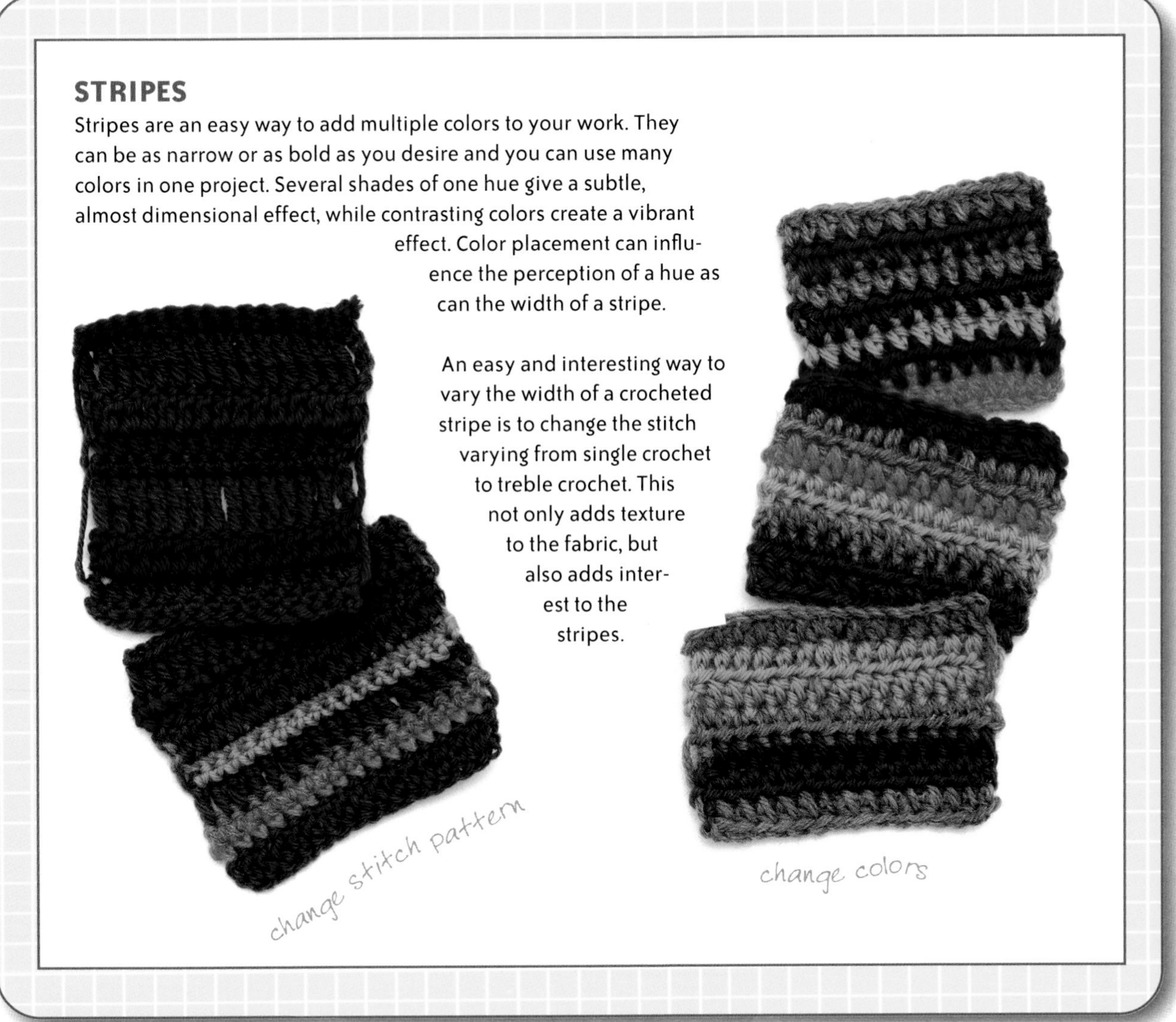

change stitch pattern

change colors

MOHAIR HATS

Starting with the soft and feminine yarn of mohair, you have many options to make this hat even more personal. Change the length and edges; make decorative flowers or other embellishments that you can pin on and change at whim. It's a woman's prerogative, isn't it?

S P E C I F I C A T I O N S

SIZE

20" (51 cm) circumference, 7½" (19 cm) long, uncuffed; 9½" (24 cm) long, cuffed, measured straight down from center top.

YARN

Bulky-weight yarn, about 75 yd (69 m) for uncuffed version, about 90 yd (82 m) for cuffed version plus about 15 yd (14 m) for edge trim, about 5 yd (4.5 m) for each flower/leaf. ***We used:*** Berroco Mohair Classic (78% mohair, 13% wool, 9% nylon; 93 yd [85 m]/43 g); Uncuffed version: 1 ball each #1138 denim blue (MC), #1136 celadon (CC). Cuffed version: 1 ball each #1108 slate gray (MC), #1136 celadon (CC). Flowers are worked in 1 ball each #1107 olive green (dark leaf), #6561 aqua heather (single flower and light leaf), #1137 teal (two-toned flower), along with scraps of both MC and CC.

HOOK

Size H/8 (5mm). Adjust hook size if necessary to obtain correct gauge.

NOTIONS

1½" (3.8 cm) pin back (optional) for each flower; tapestry needle; safety pin; sewing needle and sewing thread.

GAUGE

12 stitches and 6 rounds = 4" (10 cm) in double crochet with size H/8 (5 mm) hook.

ABBREVIATIONS

beg—begin(s), beginning
CC—contrast color
ch(s)—chain(s)
dc—double crochet
lp(s)—loop(s)
MC—main color
rep—repeat
rnd(s)—round(s)
sk—skip
sl st—slip stitch

Review Basics, page 2
Chain stitch
Double crochet
Increasing
Joining a new yarn
Marking edges
Reading a pattern
Single crochet
Slip stitch
Weaving in ends
Working in rounds

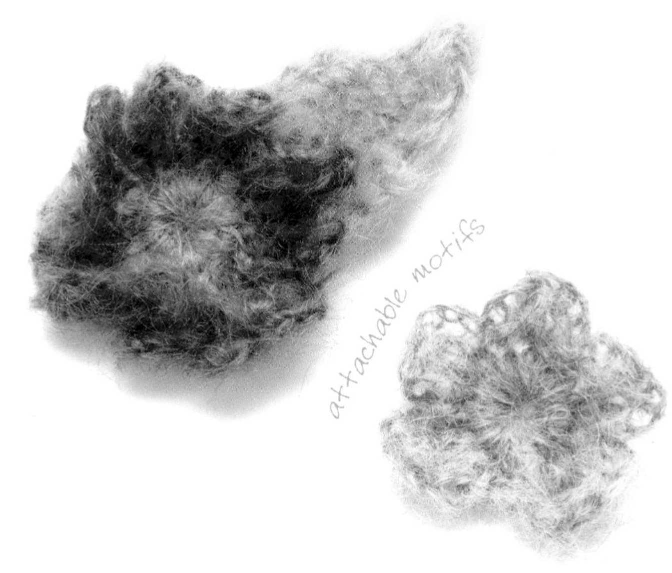

HAT

With hook and MC, ch 4 sts. Join into a ring as follows (see page 23): Insert hook into first ch and join with sl st to lp on hook.
Rnd 1: Ch 3 (counts as 1 dc), work 11 dc into the ring. Join with sl st to top of ch—12 dc.
Rnd 2: Ch 3 (for height only, does not count as dc), work 2 dc in each st (increase made) to end of rnd, join with sl st to top of ch—24 dc.

Rnd 3: Ch 3 (for height only, does not count as dc), work 1 dc in first dc, work 2 dc in next dc, *work 1 dc in next dc, work 2 dc in next dc*; rep from * to * to end of rnd, join with sl st to top of ch—36 dc.

Rnd 4: Ch 3 (for height only, does not count as dc) work 1 dc in each of first two dc, work 2 dc into next dc, *work 1 dc in each of next 2 dc, work 2 dc in next dc*; rep from * to * to end of rnd, join with sl st to top of ch—48 dc.

Rnd 5: Ch 3 (for height only, does not count as dc), work 1 dc into each of first 3 dc, work 2 dc into next dc, *work 1 dc into each of next 3 dc, work 2 dc in next dc*; rep from * to * to end of rnd, join with sl st to top of ch—60 dc.

Work even in rnds on 60 sts for a total length of 7½" (19 cm) for uncuffed version, or 9½" (24 cm) for cuffed version. Fasten off as follows: Cut yarn leaving 4" (10 cm) tail, insert tail through last lp on hook and pull to tighten and secure.

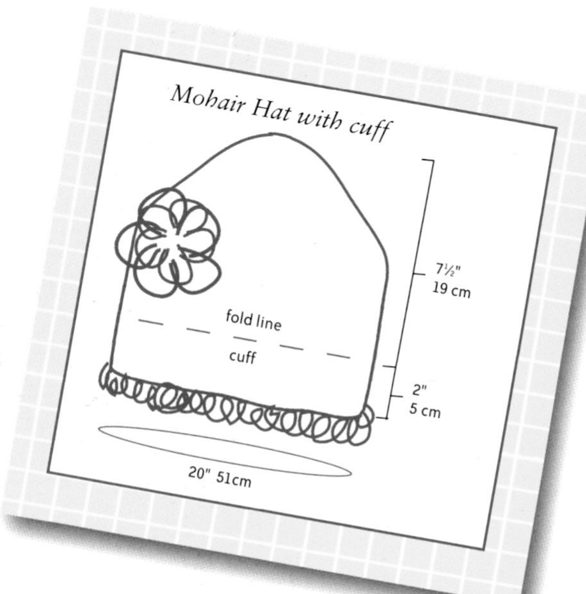

FINISHING

Thread loose yarn ends on tapestry needle and weave through sts on wrong side of work.

Scalloped edge: (uncuffed version) With hook and CC, attach yarn to center back edge of hat where rnds are joined,*sk 2 dc, work 5 dc in next dc, sk 2 dc, work 1 sc in next dc*; rep from * to * around. Fasten off.

Fringed edge: (cuffed version) With hook and CC, attach yarn at center back edge of hat where rnds are joined, *ch 4, turn. Work 1 sl st in next 3 chs (see Basics, page 5), work 1 sc in next dc*; rep from * to * around lower edge. Fasten off.

FLOWERS

Simple Flower: With hook and desired color of mohair, ch 5 sts. Join ch with sl st to form a ring.

Rnd 1: Ch 1 (counts as 1 sc), work 15 sc in ring, join with sl st to ch—16 sc.

Rnd 2: *Ch 3, work 1 dc into each of next 2 sc, ch 3, work sl st into next sc*; rep from * to * to end of round. Fasten off.

Two-Toned Flower: With hook and desired color of mohair, ch 5 sts. Join ch with sl st to form a ring. Ch 1 (counts as 1 sc), work 15 sc into ring, fasten off—16 sc. Join second color. *Ch 8, sl st into next sc*; rep from * to * to end of rnd. Fasten off.

One color is never enough

LEAF

With hook and desired color of mohair, ch 9 sts. Turn. Sk 1 ch, work 1 sc in each of next 7 sc, work 3 sc in next ch (end ch), marking center stitch of last three sts worked with contrast yarn or safety pin. Work 7 sc into opposite side of ch. Turn, ch 1, sk 1 sc, work 1 sc in each of next 7 sc, work 3 sc in next sc (marked stitch) marking center st again, work one sc in each of next 5 sc. Turn, ch 1, sk 1 sc, work 1 sc in each of next 5 sc work 3 sc in next sc (marked stitch) marking center st again, work 1 sc in each of next 5 sc. Turn. Ch 1, sk next sc, work 1 sc in each of next 5 sc, work 3 sc in next sc (marked stitch) marking center st again, work 1 sc in each of next 3 sc. Turn. Ch 1, sk next sc, work 1 sc in each of next 3 sc, work 3 sc in next sc (marked stitch), work 1 sc in each of next 3 sc. Fasten off.

Make as many flowers as you desire. Sew them to the pin back either singly or in clusters, and put them wherever you want to on the hat.

Try different colors of mohair

TWO TOO

CLOCHE

A take-off on the Roaring Twenties, this classic hat is never out of fashion. Use a yarn that drapes softly so it hugs the head, or use a stiff yarn to create a fold-back brim. Add a bit more flair to your cloche by using an openwork stitch whose flexibility adjusts to different head sizes. Whether soft or stiff, the look is haute.

SPECIFICATIONS

SIZE

23" (58.5 cm) circumference, above brim, 9" (23 cm) long, measured from center top to bottom edge.

YARN

Double-knitting weight yarn, about 250 yd (229 m). Simply Cloche: ***We used:*** Dale of Norway Sisik (30% wool, 30% mohair, 34% acrylic 65 viscose; 148 yd [136 m]/50 g): 2 balls #163 golden. Summer Cloche: ***We used:*** Rowan Linen Drape (55% linen, 45% viscose/rayon; 109 yd [100 m]/ 50 g): 3 skeins #852 salsa.

HOOK

Size F/5 (3.75 mm). Adjust hook size if necessary to obtain the correct gauge.

NOTIONS

Summer Cloche: Two decorative pony-size beads (optional); tapestry needle.

GAUGE

21 stitches and 24 rounds = 4" (10 cm) in single crochet with size F/5 (3.75 mm) hook.

ABBREVIATIONS

ch—chain
hdc—half double crochet
lp(s)—loop(s)
rep—repeat
rnd(s)—round(s)
sc—single crochet
sl st(s)—slip stitch(es)

Review Basics, page 2:
Chain stitch
Half double crochet
Increasing
Reading a pattern
Single crochet
Slip stitch
Weaving in ends
Working in rounds

SIMPLY CLOCHE

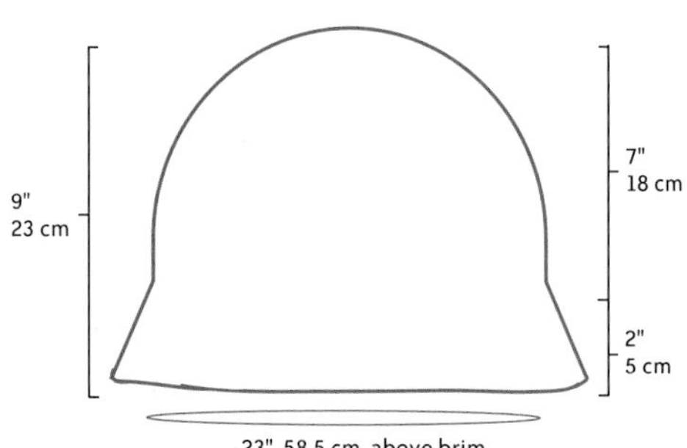

HAT

With yarn and hook, ch 4 sts. Join into a ring (see page 23) as follows: Insert hook into first ch and join with sl st to lp on hook.

Rnd 1: Ch 1 (counts as 1 sc), work 7 sc into the ring. Join rnd with sl st to top of ch—8 sts.

Rnd 2: Ch 1, work 2 sc in each sc to end of rnd. Join rnd with sl st to top of ch—16 sts.

Rnd 3: Ch 1, work sc in each st to end of rnd. Join rnd with sl st to top of ch.

Rnd 4: Ch 1, *work 1 sc in first sc, work 2 sc in next sc*; rep from * to * to end of rnd. Join rnd with sl st to top of ch—24 sts.

Rnd 5: Rep Rnd 3.

Rnd 6: Ch 1, *work 1 sc in each of next 2 sc, work 2 sc in next sc*; rep from * to * to end of rnd. Join rnd with sl st to top of ch—32 sts.

Rnd 7: Rep Rnd 3.

Rnd 8: Ch 1, *work 1 sc in each of next 3 sc, work 2 sc in next sc*; rep from * to * to end of rnd. Join rnd with sl st to top of ch—40 sts.

Rnd 9: Rep Rnd 3.

Rnd 10: Ch 1, *work 1 sc in each of next 4 sc, work 2 sc in next sc*; rep from * to * to end of rnd. Join rnd with sl st to top of ch—48 sts.

Rnd 11: Rep Rnd 3.

Rnd 12: Ch 1, *work 1 sc in each of next 5 sc, work 2 sc in next sc*; rep from * to * to end of rnd. Join rnd with sl st to top of ch—56 sts.

Rnd 13: Rep Rnd 3.

Rnd 14: Ch 1, * work 1 sc in each of next 6 sc, work 2 sc in next sc*; rep from * to * to end of rnd. Join rnd with sl st to top of ch—64 sts.

Rnd 15: Rep Rnd 3.

Rnd 16: Ch 1, *work 1 sc in each of next 7 sc, work 2 sc in next sc*; rep from * to * to end of rnd. Join rnd with sl st to top of ch—72 sts.

Rnd 17: Rep Rnd 3.

Rnd 18: Ch 1, *work 1 sc in each of next 8 sc, work 2 sc in next sc*; rep from * to * to end of rnd. Join rnd with sl st to top of ch—80 sts.

a soft, tweedy yarn

Rnd 19: Rep Rnd 3.
Rnd 20: Ch 1, *work 1 sc in each of next 9 sc, work 2 sc in next sc*; rep from * to * to end of rnd. Join rnd with sl st to top of ch—88 sts.
Rnd 21: Rep Rnd 3.
Rnd 22: Ch 1, *work 1 sc in each of next 10 sc, work 2 sc in next sc*; rep from * to * to end of rnd. Join rnd with sl st to top of ch—96 sts.
Rnd 23: Rep Rnd 3.
Rnd 24: Ch 1, *work 1 sc in each of next 11 sc, work 2 sc in next sc*; rep from * to * to end of rnd. Join rnd with sl st to top of ch—104 sts.
Rnd 25: Rep Rnd 3.
Rnd 26: Ch 1, *work 1 sc in each of next 12 sc, work 2 sc in next sc*; rep from * to * to end of rnd. Join rnd with sl st to top of ch—112 sts.
Rnds 27–28: Ch 1, *work 1 sc in each of next 13 sc, work 2 sc in next sc*; rep from * to * to end of rnd. Join rnd with sl st to top of ch—120 sts.
Rnd 29: Rep Rnd 3.
Work should measure about 5" (12.5 cm) in length from top of crown, and about 23" (58.5 cm) around the perimeter. Rep Rnd 29, working without further increases, until hat measures 7" (18 cm) in length, measuring straight down from the beginning circle to edge of brim.

Shape brim:
Rnd 1: Ch 1, *work 1 sc in each of next 2 sc, work 2 sc in next sc*; rep from * to * to end of rnd. Join with sl st to top of ch—160 sts.
Rnd 2: Ch 1, *work 1 sc in each of next 9 sc, work 2 sc in next sc*; rep from * to * to end of rnd. Join with sl st to top of ch—176 sts.
Next 8 rnds: Work sc in each st, without further increases.
Fasten off as follows: Cut yarn leaving 4" (10 cm) tail, insert tail through last lp on hook and pull to tighten and secure.

FINISHING

Thread loose ends on tapestry needle and weave through sts on wrong side of work. Steam lightly as needed.

SHAPING

Since crochet lends itself naturally to graceful shaping, it's an ideal medium for sculptural forms as well as garments and accessories with a defined structural presence. Because each stitch is a unit in and of itself, it is easy to produce a shape or form by inserting a stitch wherever needed without disturbing the stitches already created.

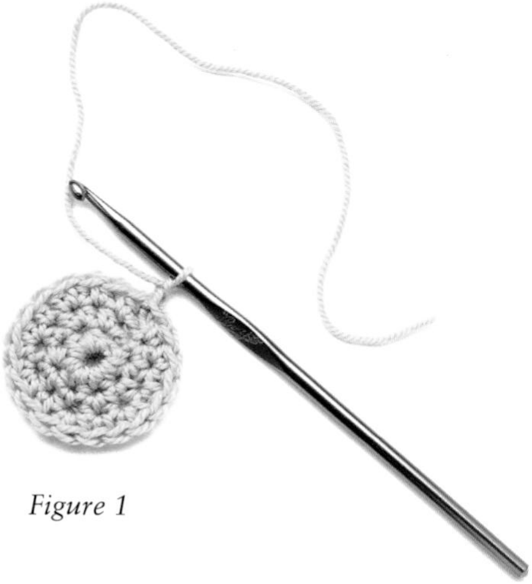

Figure 1

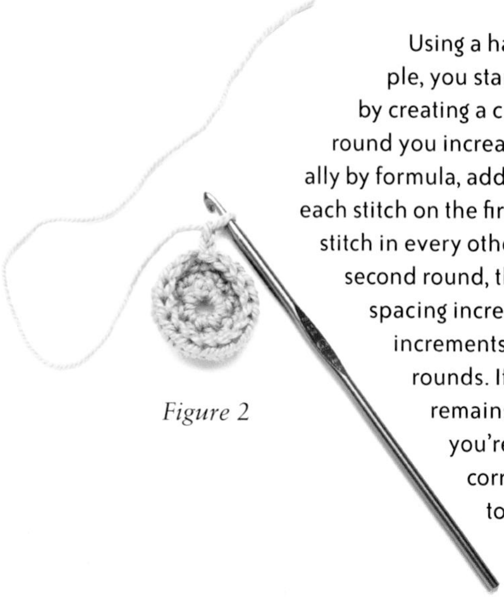

Figure 2

Using a hat as an example, you start at the crown by creating a circle. Round by round you increase stitches, usually by formula, adding one stitch in each stitch on the first round, one stitch in every other stitch in the second round, then gradually spacing increases in even increments on subsequent rounds. If the piece remains a flat circle, you're following the correct rate of increase (Figure 1). The circle curving inward indicates too few increase stitches; you should add more stitches per round (Figure 2). If the circle starts to ripple, there are too many increases; correct by increasing fewer stitches per round or by working even rounds between increase rounds (Figure 3). When the circle reaches the desired diameter for the top of the head, simply stop increasing and begin to work even. After a round or two, the piece will start to curve inward and the hat will take shape. At this point you're creating a cylinder. A stocking cap can end at the desired length. To create a brimmed hat, the increase process starts again at the bottom. Crochet can really take on any form you desire. In the case of the hat, everything is spaced evenly to create a symmetrical form. By concentrating increases or decreases in specific areas, you can produce organic, irregular shapes (see Organic Baskets, page 102).

Figure 3

SUMMER CLOCHE

HAT

Work as for basic Simply Cloche until hat measures 6" (15 cm) in length, measuring straight down from starting ring at crown top to bottom edge.

Openwork rnd: Ch 2, *work 1 hdc in next sc, ch 1, sk next sc*; rep from * to * to end of rnd. Join rnd with sl st to top of ch.

Next rnd: Work even in sc working 1 sc in each hdc and 1 sc in each ch-1 space.

Next rnd: Work even in sc to end of rnd.

Next rnd: Rep Openwork rnd.

Shape brim same as for Simply Cloche.

CORD

Ch 240. Turn (Figure 1). Beg with the second chain from hook, work 1 sl st in each ch (Figure 2). Continue across row until complete (Figure 3). Fasten off as follows: Cut yarn leaving 4" (10 cm) tail, insert tail through last lp on hook and pull to tighten and secure.

FINISHING

Work in loose ends. Thread cord through lower openwork round. Attach bead to each end of cord and knot end of cord to hold it in place.

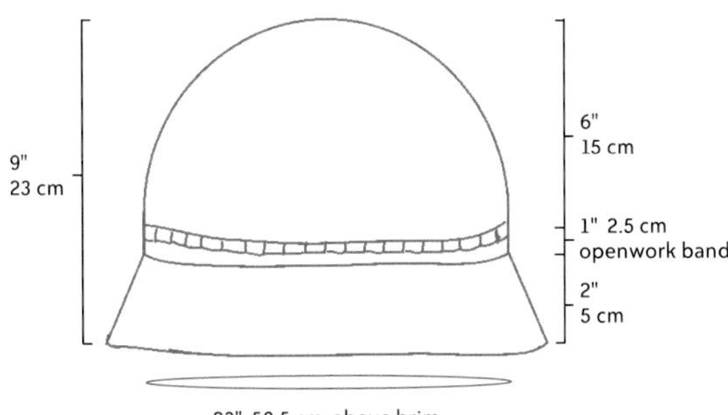

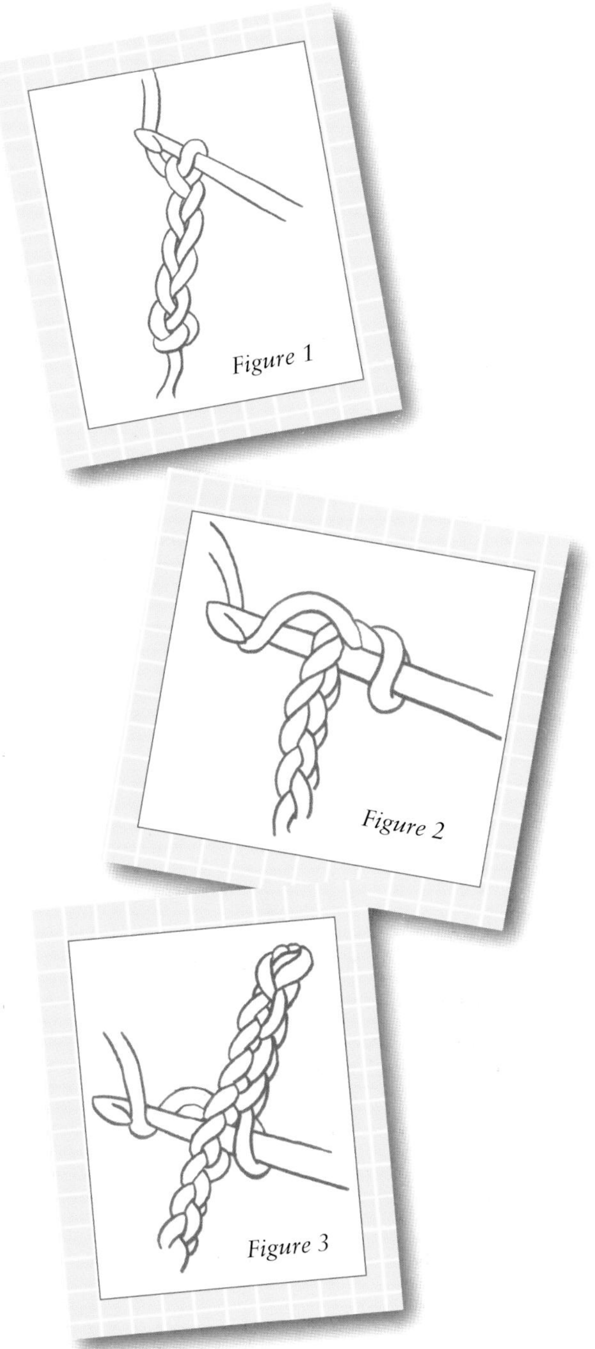

Figure 1

Figure 2

Figure 3

ZIGZAG

SCARF

This is no ho-hum ripple stitch. Turn the stitch horizontally, add just the right edge trim, and you have a scarf with great dramatic flair.

S P E C I F I C A T I O N S

SIZE

8½" (21.5 cm) wide × 57" (145 cm) long, excluding trim.

YARN

Worsted-weight yarn, about 138 yd (123 m) each of 5 colors. ***We used:*** Classic Elite Waterspun (felted 100% merino wool; 138 yd [123 m]/50 g): 1 skein each #5036 celery (A), # 5031 turquoise (B), #5035 fern green (C), #5072 light teal (D), #5039 camel (E).

HOOK

Size H/8 (5 mm). Adjust hook size if necessary to obtain the correct gauge.

NOTIONS

Tapestry needle.

GAUGE

23 stitches and 14 rows = 4" (10 cm) in ripple stitch with size H/8 (5 mm) hook.

ABBREVIATIONS

ch(s)—chain(s)
dc—double crochet
lp(s)—loop(s)
rep—repeat
sc—single crochet
sk—skip
st(s)—stitch(es)
sl st—slip stitch

Review Basics, page 2:
Chain stitch
Reading a pattern
Single crochet
Weaving in ends

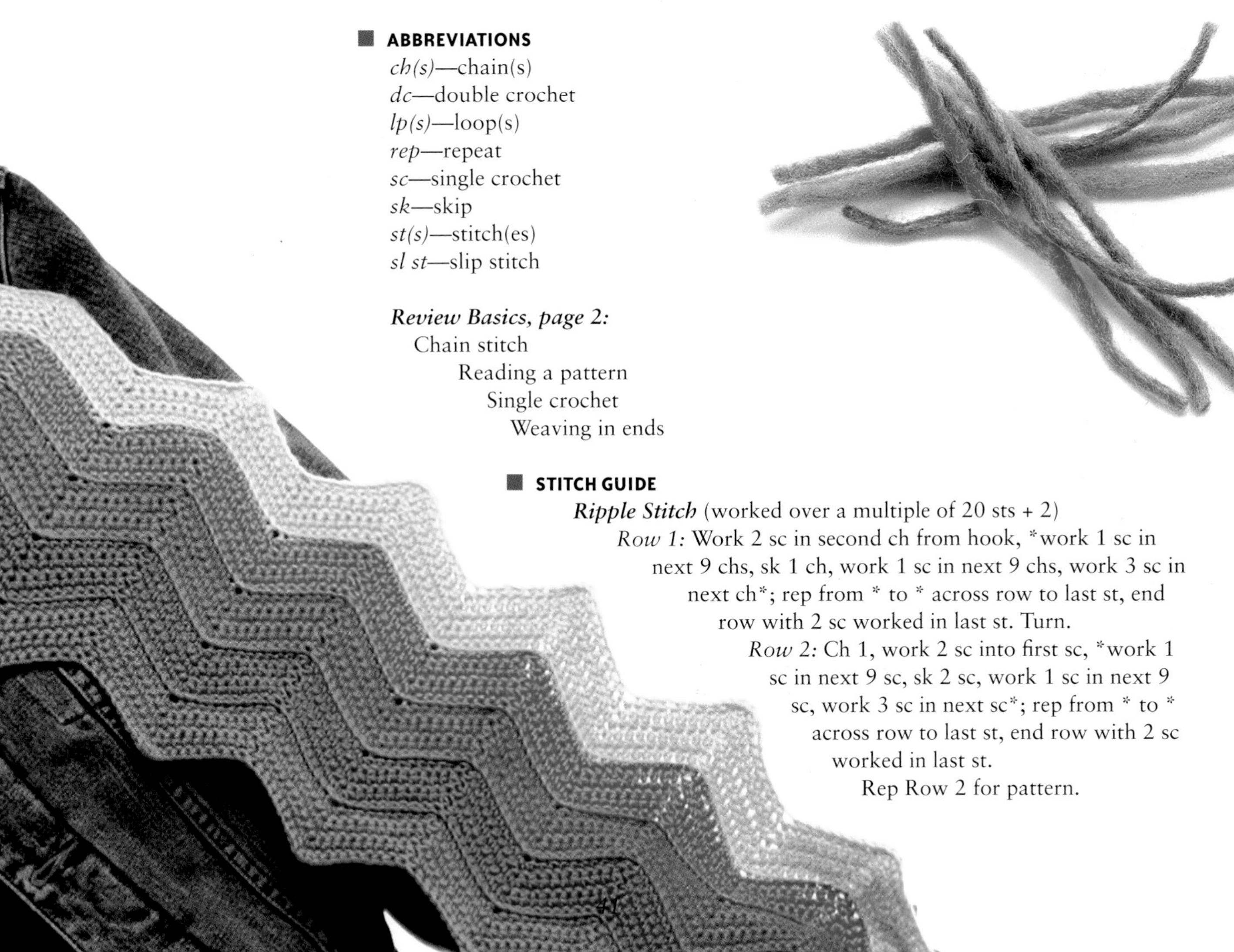

STITCH GUIDE

Ripple Stitch (worked over a multiple of 20 sts + 2)

Row 1: Work 2 sc in second ch from hook, *work 1 sc in next 9 chs, sk 1 ch, work 1 sc in next 9 chs, work 3 sc in next ch*; rep from * to * across row to last st, end row with 2 sc worked in last st. Turn.

Row 2: Ch 1, work 2 sc into first sc, *work 1 sc in next 9 sc, sk 2 sc, work 1 sc in next 9 sc, work 3 sc in next sc*; rep from * to * across row to last st, end row with 2 sc worked in last st.

Rep Row 2 for pattern.

SCARF

With hook and color A, loosely ch 322 sts. Work 6 rows in ripple stitch. On next row, (right side of work) change to color B (see Basics, page 6) and working into the back loop only (Figure), work 1 row ripple stitch. Work 5 more rows in ripple stitch as previously established (working through both lps). Work 6 rows each in colors C, D, and E, working the first row of each color in the back lp only as described for color B, for a total of 30 rows. Fasten off as follows: Cut yarn leaving 4" (10 cm) tail, insert tail through last st on hook and pull to tighten and secure.

FINISHING

With wrong side of work facing and color A at right-hand edge of the short, straight edge, attach color A in corner stitch, and make Corkscrew Fringe: *Ch 20, work 1 dc in third ch from hook, 3 dc in each of next 12 chs, 1 hdc in next ch, 1 sc in next ch, 1 sl st in each of next 3 chs. Work 6 sc evenly along edge using the same color as the stripe*. Change to color B and rep from * to *. Rep sequence for remaining colors—5 corkscrew fringes. Rep for opposite short edge of scarf, reversing color sequence to work corkscrews in the same colors as the corresponding stripe. Fasten off. Thread loose ends on tapestry needle and weave through sts on wrong side of work. Steam lightly.

CORKSCREW FRINGE

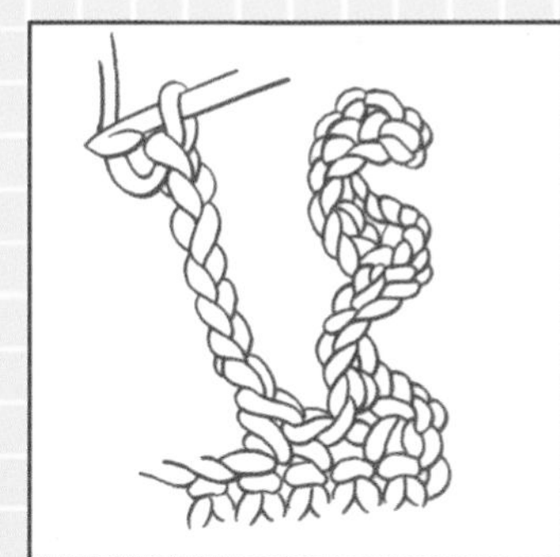

Used as edging or embellishment, corkscrew fringe is a fun, whimsical addition to a crocheted item. It looks much more complicated than it actually is. You basically "overload" a chain with stitches, usually working three stitches back into each chain. As the stitches crowd into the chain they are forced into a spiral and the corkscrew is created.

Based on the length of the original chain and choice of stitch, the corkscrew can be a slender tendril or a fat ringlet. A single crochet will produce a slender corkscrew, double crochet a more substantial one.

To make a slender corkscrew, attach the yarn and chain about twenty to twenty-five stitches. Work one stitch in the first chain and two stitches in each subsequent chain. Fasten off or, if you are creating a row of fringe, continue on to the next corkscrew working stitches in between as desired (Figure 1). For a thick corkscrew, chain twenty stitches. Work one double crochet in the third chain from the hook. Work three double crochet in each of the next twelve chains. Work one half double crochet in the next chain, one single crochet in the next chain, slip-stitch in each of the next three chains. Fasten off or continue to the next corkscrew (Figure 2). For a corkscrew that curls close to the garment, work three stitches in each chain back to the beginning instead of tapering to fewer, shorter stitches.

Personalize your edge trim by playing with chain length, stitch choice, and corkscrew placement.

Figure 1

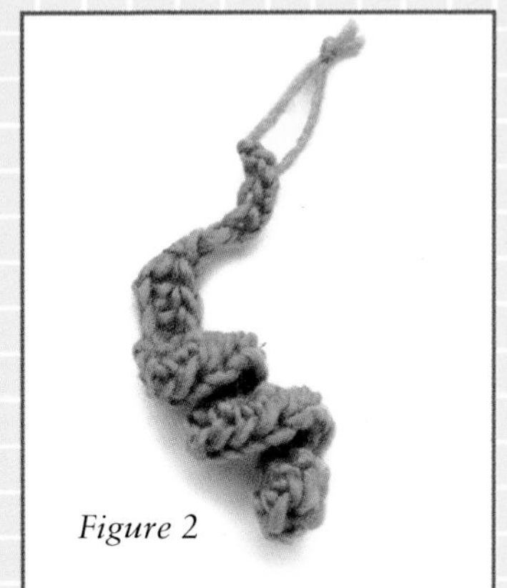

Figure 2

KALEIDOSCOPE

SCARF

You can have it all with this scarf—the intricacy of modular motifs, the softest, most delicate yarn imaginable, and vibrant color combinations that are both gossamer and bold. Wrap the scarf around your neck and you'll be petted to a fare-thee-well.

SPECIFICATIONS

SIZE	YARN	HOOK	NOTIONS	GAUGE
About 7" (18 cm) wide, 60" (152.5 cm) long after blocking.	Laceweight mohair, about 750 yds (692 m). ***We used:*** K1C2 Douceur et Soie (70% baby mohair, 30% silk; 225 yd [205 m]/25 g). 1 ball each #8243 soft sunrise (A), #8248 velvet rose (B), #8352 coral (C), #8249 deep garnet (D), #8254 burgundy (E).	Size B/1 (2.25 mm). Adjust hook size if necessary to obtain the correct gauge.	Tapestry needle.	One motif = 2 1¼" (6.5 cm) square before blocking, with size B/1 (2.25 mm) hook.

ABBREVIATIONS

ch(s)—chain(s)
dc—double crochet
dc 2tog—double crochet 2 stitches together. *Wrap the yarn around the hook, insert hook into next stitch (or as pattern designates), wrap yarn around hook, draw up loop, wrap yarn around hook, draw through 2 loops,* (2 loops left on hook), repeat from * to * (3 loops left on hook), wrap yarn around hook again and draw through all 3 loops, completing stitch.
dc 3tog—double crochet 3 stitches together. Same as dc 2tog, but with repeat from * to * 2 times (4 loops left on hook), wrap yarn around hook again and draw through all 4 loops, completing stitch.
lp(s)—loop(s)
rep—repeat
rnd—round
sc—single crochet
sl st—slip stitch
sp—space
st(s)—stitch(es)

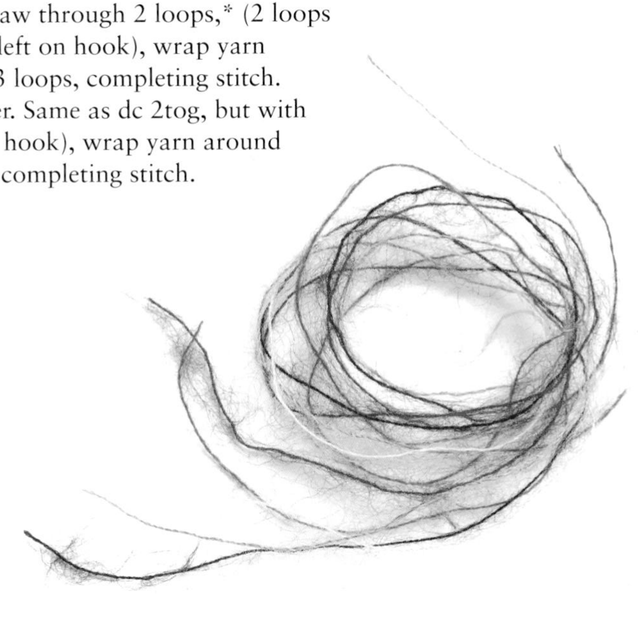

Review Basics, page 2:
Blocking
Chain stitch
Double crochet
Reading a pattern
Slip stitch
Weaving in ends

use a fine silk

SCARF

The scarf is made up of 40 repeats of the Sow Thistle Square Motif—8 squares each, worked in five different color combinations. For each motif the colors are separated as follows: Use the first color to make the foundation chain and work Round 1. Change to the second color and work Round 2. Change to the third color and work Rounds 3 and 4.

CREATING MOTIFS

Motifs form the basis of modular crochet and offer versatility in design, shape, color, and texture. From a practical standpoint, motifs make big crocheted pieces portable without your feeling engulfed by them. Motifs also provide an easy way to vary colors and add interest to a total piece.

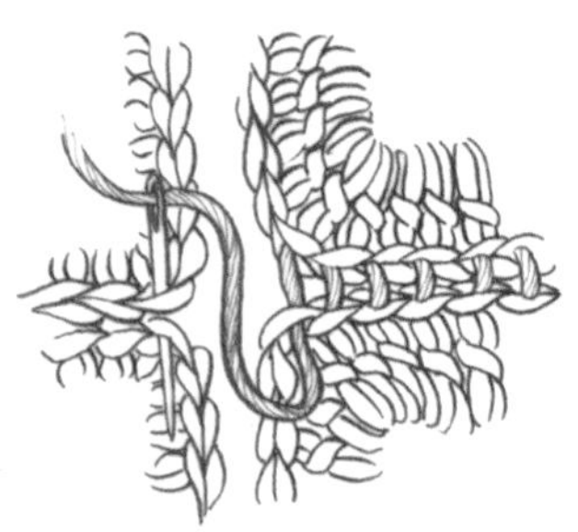

Figure 1

Although motifs can take on any finished form from geometric granny squares to organic shapes like flowers, they all begin from a circle which, within a series of rounds, is transformed into a square, hexagon, or triangle. For the designer, the challenge within this shape change is to create a pleasing pattern that balances increases per round with decorative stitches to keep the work from rippling or curling while it maintains design integrity.

The next challenge is joining the motifs into one unified fabric. Motifs can be completed and sewed together, usually with a whipstitch (Figure 1). This method works best when the motif has straight sides that can be easily aligned; the typical granny square is an example. When a motif has lacy edges, it is more easily crocheted together by working the first motif in its entirety, and then joining motifs as you work. You can also join elements by crocheting them together with a chain that alternately slip stitches to adjacent motifs at regular intervals, thereby creating a lacy effect that becomes part of the design (Figure 2).

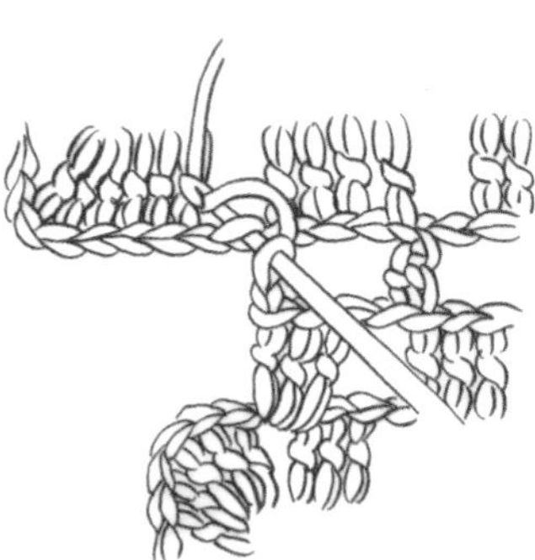

Figure 2

FOR MOTIF COLORS AND OVERALL COLOR PLACEMENT

Motif 1—colors A (first color), B (second color), C (third color)
Motif 2—colors B (first color), C (second color), D (third color)
Motif 3—colors C (first color), D (second color), E (third color)
Motif 4—colors D (first color), E (second color), A (third color)
Motif 5—colors E (first color), A (second color), B (third color)

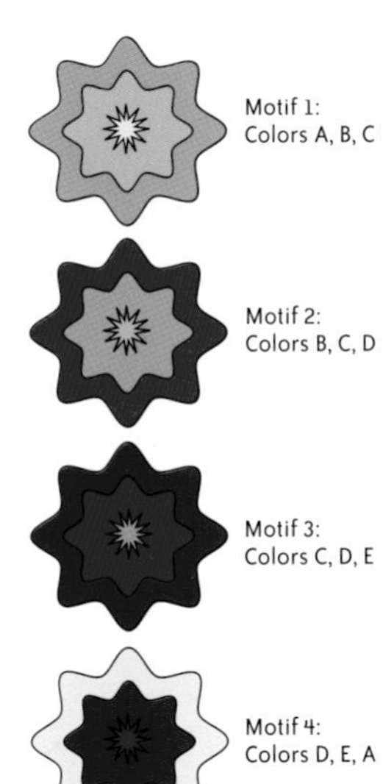

1	2
4	3
5	1
3	2
4	5
1	2
4	3
5	1
3	2
4	5
1	2
4	3
5	1
3	2
4	5
1	2
4	3
5	1
3	2
4	5

60" 152.5 cm Measurement includes border edging

7" 18 cm

SOW THISTLE SQUARE MOTIF

Foundation Ring: Use the first color of the motif being worked, ch 4 sts, join with sl st to form a ring.

Rnd 1: Ch 4 (counts as 1 dc and 1 ch), work (1 dc, ch 1) 11 times into the ring, sl st to third st of ch 4. Fasten off as follows: Cut yarn leaving 4" (10 cm) tail, insert tail through last lp on hook and pull to tighten.

Rnd 2: With second color, join yarn into ch sp, ch 3, dc 2tog in same sp (counts as dc 3tog), (ch 3, dc 3tog into next space) 11 times, ch 3, sl st to top of first cluster. Fasten off.

Rnd 3: With third color, join yarn into ch-3 sp, ch 1, 1 sc in same sp, (ch 5, 1.sc into next ch-3 sp) 11 times, ch 2, 1 dc into first sc.

Rnd 4: Continuing with third color, ch 1, 1 sc into same ch-5 sp, *ch 5, sc 1 into next ch-5 sp, ch 1, [5 dc, ch 3, 5 dc] into next ch-5 sp, ch 1, sc 1 into next ch-5 sp*; rep from * to * 3 more times omitting sc 1 at the end of last rep, sl st to first sc to join. Fasten off.

Beginning at one end of the placement chart, work the motifs following the chart. The motifs are joined together at the corners and midpoints when working the final round of each motif. **Note:** First motif is worked in its entirety but subsequent motifs are joined during the last round. To join motifs, on Rnd 4 attach at corners by inserting the hook through corner sp of the previous motif before completing ch 3, and at the side centers by inserting the hook through ch-5 sp of previous motif before completing ch 5.

FINISHING

Border:

Rnd 1: With right side of work facing, attach color B at upper right-hand corner with sl st. Work 1 sc over sl st, *ch 5, sk 3 ch or sts, sc 1 into next st or ch, working into half of ch or entire st accordingly*; rep from * to * around edge of scarf, adjusting the chains if necessary so that there is a ch 1 in each corner, end rnd with ch 2, 1 dc in first sc.

Rnd 2: Ch 3, work 6 dc in same sp, *ch 1, work 1 sc in next ch-5 sp, ch 1, work 7 dc in next ch-5 sp*; rep from * to * around edge, working corners as follows: On last ch-5 sp per side work 7 dc, ch 3, work 7 dc in first ch-5 sp of next side. Continue working as established around the scarf edge. Complete the rnd by working ch 1, then 1 dc in top of starting ch. Fasten off.

Rnd 3: Attach color D at corner sp. Ch 3, work 6 dc in same sp, *ch 1, work 1 sc in fourth dc of previous row, ch 1, work 7 dc in sc from previous row*; rep from * to * around entire edge of scarf, and working (7 dc, ch 3, 7 dc) in the same space at each corner; end rnd with 7 dc, ch 3, attach to top of beg ch with sl st. Fasten off. Weave in loose ends and block.

RETRO

BED SLIPPERS

The inspiration may be vintage, but this handpainted yarn is really up-to-date and makes these slippers extraordinary. You'll want to have them cuddling your feet as soon as you get in the door.

SPECIFICATIONS

SIZE

To fit a woman's medium foot, 9–10" (23–25.5 cm) from tip of heel to tip of toe.

YARN

Fingering-weight yarn, about 300 yd (275 m).
We used: Koigu Painter's Palette Premium Merino (100% merino wool; 175 yd [160 m]/50 g): 2 skeins #P113.

HOOK

Size C/2 (3 mm). Adjust hook size if necessary to obtain the correct gauge.

NOTIONS

Two yards (1.83 m) ribbon 1½–2" (3.8–5 cm) wide; tapestry needle.

GAUGE

18 stitches = 3.25" (8.5 cm) and 6 rows = 2.5" (6.5 cm) in Sweetpea Stitch with size C/2 (3 mm) hook. 20 stitches = 3.25" (8.5 cm) and 8 rows = 3.5" (9 cm) in double crochet with size C/2 (3 mm) hook.

ABBREVIATIONS

beg—begin(s), beginning
bet—between
ch(s)—chain(s)
dc—double crochet
patt—pattern
rep—repeat
rnd(s)—round(s)
sc—single crochet
sk—skip
sl st(s)—slip stitch(es)
st(s)—stitch(es)

Review Basics, page 2:
Chain stitch
Double crochet
Increasing
Reading a pattern
Single crochet
Working between stitches
Weaving in ends

a yarn of many colors

PATTERN STITCH

Sweetpea Stitch: Worked over a multiple of 7 + 4 plus a turning ch of 3 sts.
Row 1: Work 1 dc in fourth ch from hook, *sk 2 chs, 5 dc in next ch, sk 2 chs, 1 dc in each of next 2 chs*; rep from * to * to last ch 3 chs, sk 2 chs, work 3 dc in last ch. Ch 3, turn work.
Row 2: Work 1 dc in space bet first 2 dc of previous row, *work 5 dc in space bet the 2 single dc, 1 dc in space bet second and third dc of 5-dc cluster, 1 dc in space bet third and fourth dc of 5-dc cluster*; rep from * to * across row to turning ch, end row with 3 dc in the space bet the last dc and the turning ch. Ch 3, turn.
Repeat Row 2 for patt.

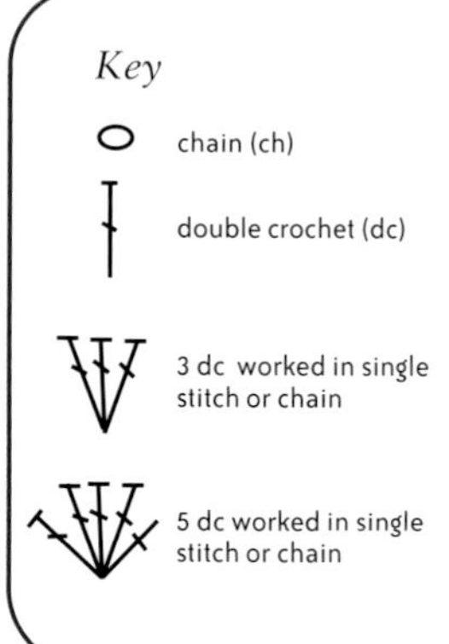

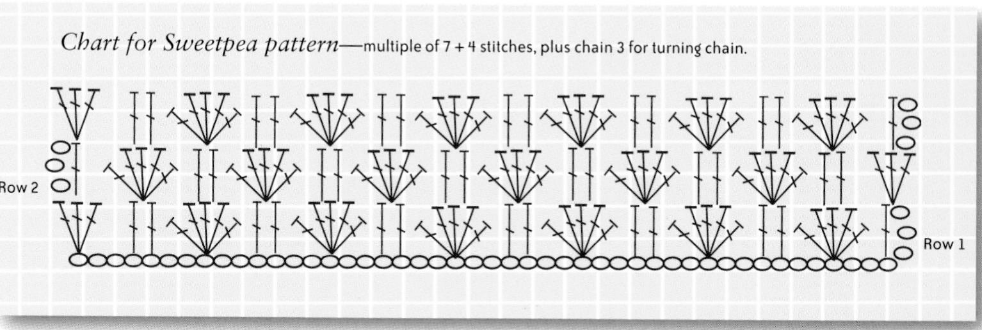

Chart for Sweetpea pattern—multiple of 7 + 4 stitches, plus chain 3 for turning chain.

BED SLIPPERS

Starting at toe, with hook and yarn, ch 4 sts, join into a ring (see page 23) as follows: Insert hook into first ch made and join to lp on hook with sl st to form the ring.

Rnd 1: Ch 3 (counts as 1 dc), work 9 dc in ring, join rnd with sl st to top of ch 3—10 dc.

Rnd 2: Ch 3 (counts as 1 dc), work 1 dc in first dc, work 2 dc in each of next 9 dc, join rnd with sl st to top of ch 3—20 dc.

Rnd 3: Ch 3 (counts as 1 dc), sk first dc, *work 2 dc in next dc, work 1 dc in next dc*; rep from * to * to last st, work 2 dc in last dc, join rnd with sl st to top of ch—30 dc.

Rnd 4: Ch 3 (counts as 1 dc), sk first dc, *2 dc in next dc, 1 dc in each of next 2 dc*; rep from * to * to last 2 sts, work 2 dc in next dc, 1 dc in last st, join rnd with sl st to top of ch—40 dc.

Rnd 5: Ch 3 (counts as 1 dc), sk first dc, work 1 dc in each dc to end of rnd, join rnd with sl st to top of ch 3.

Rnd 6: Ch 3 (counts as 1 dc), sk first dc, work 1 dc in next dc, *work 2 dc in next dc, work 1 dc in each of next 3 dc*; rep from * to * to last 2 sts, work 2 dc in next st, work 1 dc in last st, join rnd with sl st to top of ch—50 dc.

Work even in rnds as established on 50 dc until work measures 4" (10 cm) from beg chain at toe. Fasten off as follows: Cut yarn leaving 4" (10 cm) tail, insert tail through last lp on hook and pull to tighten.

With right side of work facing, reattach yarn at 25th st from where rnds join. Ch 3. **Note:** The Sweetpea patt is worked flat, back and forth, turning the work at the end of each row. Work Row 1 of Sweetpea patt over next 46 sts (4 dc sts from the previous rnd remain unworked). Turn, ch 3. Work Row 2 of Sweetpea patt. Rep Row 2 until the Sweetpea section measures 6" (15 cm) in length, or until both sections (dc and Sweetpea patt) measure the desired foot length. Ch 1, turn bed slipper inside out. Fold edge in half lengthwise and seam back edges together with sl st crochet. Cut yarn leaving 4" (10 cm) tail to weave in later.

FINISHING

Turn slipper right side out.

Rnd 1: Attach yarn at top of heel seam, ch 1, work 60 sc evenly spaced around opening edge, join rnd with sl st.

Rnd 2: Ch 3 (for height only, does not count as st), work 1 dc in first sc, *ch 2, sk 2 sc, work 1 dc in each of next 2 sc*; rep from * to * to last st, end rnd with 1 dc, join rnd to top of ch 3.

Rnd 3: Ch 1, work 1 sc in each st or ch to end of rnd, join rnd with slip stitch to ch 1—60 sts.

Rnd 4: *Sk 2 sts, work 5 dc in next sc, sk next 2 sc, work 1 sc in next sc*; rep from * to * to end of rnd, join rnd with sl st. Fasten off.

With tapestry needle, weave in loose yarn tails to wrong side of work, thread through several sts to secure ends. Weave one yard (91.5 cm) length of ribbon through dc spaces in Rnd 2, folding ribbon to fit through spaces. Tie large bow at front.

READING CHARTS

There is an international language of crochet symbols that appears in the form of charts and graphs. If you learn to identify these symbols and read the charts, you can work with patterns written in any language. In addition, charts can really help you conceptualize a pattern, whereas words may be ambiguous.

The method for working with charts is very logical; they're read in the way you work the pattern. Motif charts are read from the center out. For fabrics worked back and forth in rows, Row 1 is at the bottom of the chart. Odd-numbered rows are read from right to left and even-numbered rows are read from left to right. The placement of the row number on the side of the chart indicates the direction in which you are to read—odd numbers appear on the right-hand side of the chart and even numbers appear on the left-hand side. Symbols are relative to stitch size. A chain or slip-stitch symbol appears as a small oval, open or closed, while symbols for single, half double, double, and treble crochet stitches are progressively longer variations of the same symbol. Special abbreviations are indicated by a unique symbol included with the pattern.

Since charts clarify stitch placement, they are especially helpful when you're crocheting lacy or openwork patterns that can easily be thrown off by a misplaced stitch. Although reading charts can appear daunting at first, it is well worth mastering. The skill will encourage versatility in your crochet abilities and help simplify written instructions.

- ○ chain (ch)
- ● slip stitch (sl st)
- + single crochet (sc)
- half double crochet (hdc)
- double crochet (dc)
- treble crochet (tr)
- double treble crochet (dtr)
- two double crochets (trebles) worked in a single stitch
- three double crochets (trebles) worked in a single stitch
- four double crochets (trebles) worked in a single stitch
- five double crochets (trebles) worked in a single stitch
- five loop popcorn
- five loop puff stitch
- five loop cluster
- picot of chain three

GOOD VIBRATIONS

BAG

Here's a bag that's almost foolproof to make. The pattern stitch pretty much disappears when the bag is felted, so use stripes or wild combos to put the emphasis on color.

S P E C I F I C A T I O N S

SIZE	YARN	HOOK	NOTIONS	GAUGE
About 14" (35.5 cm) wide × 10" (25.5 cm) high × 6" (15 cm) deep. Strap is about 31" (79 cm) long.	Worsted-weight wool, about 900 yd (830 m). ***We used:*** Brown Sheep Lamb's Pride Worsted (85% wool, 15% mohair; 190 yd [173 m]/113 g): 1 skein each M-05 onyx (A), M-140 aran (B), M-180 ruby red (C), M-185 aubergine (D), M-29 Jack's plum (E), M-67 loden leaf (F), M-113 oregano (G), M-190 jaded dream (H), M-42 twilight green (I).	Size K/10½ (6.5 mm). Adjust hook size if necessary to obtain the correct gauge.	Tapestry needle; safety pins, or long straight sewing pins with colored heads; two decorative buttons about 1½" (3.8 cm) in diameter, sewing thread to coordinate with buttons; sewing needle; zippered king-size cotton pillow protector for felting; mild laundry soap.	12 stitches and 12 rows = 4" (10 cm) in single crochet using size K/10½ (6.5 mm) hook before felting; 14½ stitches and 16 rows = 4" (10 cm) after felting.

Note: Felting is not an exact science. Individual felting results will vary (see Felting, page 55). It is best to go slowly and repeat the process as many times as necessary to achieve the desired results. The felting process was repeated three times with the bag shown here.

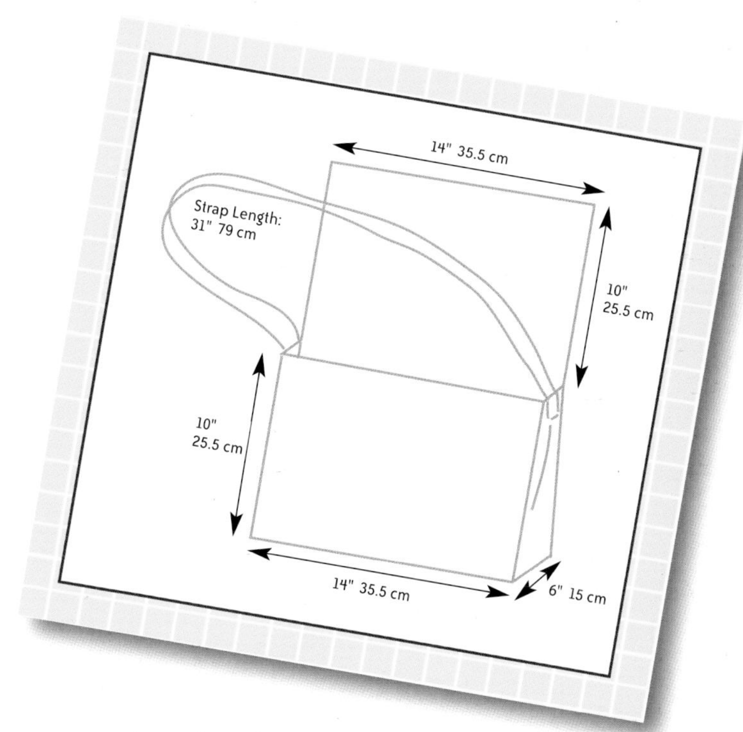

ABBREVIATIONS

ch—chain
lp(s)—loop(s)
rep—repeat
sc—single crochet
st(s)—stitch(es)

Review Basics, page 2:
Chain stitch
Reading a pattern
Single crochet
Seaming

STRIPE PATTERN SEQUENCE FOR FRONT/BACK/FLAP

3 rows C	1 row C
1 row D	3 rows D
3 rows E	1 row E
1 row F	3 rows F
3 rows G	1 row G
1 row H	3 rows H
3 rows I	1 row I

Important Note: Do not weave in the yarn tails when you're changing colors. Leave about 3" (7.5 cm) beginning or ending a color and knot the yarn tails together close to the edge of the work using a square knot. The yarn tails will form the fringe along the edges of the bag when it's felted. Crocheting over the yarn tails to secure them will cause uneven stripes and distorted felt.

FRONT/BACK/FLAP

The front, back, and flap are made in one continuous piece. With hook and color A, loosely ch 52 sts. Work 1 row sc over 51 sts. Continuing in sc, work the 28-row stripe pattern (see Changing Colors, page 17) sequence for a total of 5 times (140 rows). Change to color A and work 1 more row in sc. Fasten off as follows: Cut yarn leaving 3" (7.5 cm) tail, insert tail through last lp on hook and pull to tighten.

SIDE PANELS

(Make 2) With hook and color A, loosely ch 37 sts. *Continuing with color A, work 3 rows sc. Change to color B and work 3 rows sc*. Rep from * to * 3 more times—24 rows total. Fasten off.

STRAP

With hook and color A, loosely ch 102 sts. Continuing with color A, sc 3 rows. Change to color B and sc 3 rows. Rejoin color A and sc 3 rows. Fasten off. ***Strap anchor:*** With hook and color C, work 8 sc sts evenly across one short edge of strap. Continue with color C and sc 8 more rows. Fasten off. Make another anchor at the second short edge of strap. With tapestry needle, weave in all loose strap yarn tails to the wrong side of work. These yarn tails are not included in the side fringes.

FINISHING

The bag is assembled with the seam allowance and fringing visible on the right side of the fabric. With wrong sides of work together, pin the front/ back/flap piece to the side panels, fitting around two long sides of side panel and one short side. The remainder becomes the bag flap. Make sure that all yarn ends are on the outside—right side—of the bag. With color A, slip-stitch crochet pieces together, working the seam about one stitch from the edges. **Note:** If you desire a cleaner look, without fringing and exposed seams, pin the right sides of the bag together when you seam, with the yarn tail fringes pushed through to the wrong side of the work. Trim yarn tails after felting.

Place the bag in a zippered pillowcase along with the strap, then felt to measurements or desired firmness and density (see Felting, page 55). When the felting is finished, and both the bag and strap are completely dry, finish the bag as follows: Make a pleat in upper edge of the side panel by folding the side panel lengthwise at its center; with threaded needle, backstitch 1½" (3.8 cm) down from the top edge of the side panel. Pin the strap anchor—red square—over the pleat, and centered between the side panel edges. With color A, stitch around both sides and across the top of the red anchor square attaching it firmly to the side panel over the top of the pleat. Repeat the pleat and strap anchor attachment instructions on the second side panel. Remove all pins. Place a decorative button on top of the red anchor square, and with threaded needle, stitch the button securely through all the fabric layers. Repeat with second button on the other side panel.

FELTING

Felting is a process of fulling a wool fiber to produce a thicker, denser fabric with a soft finish. Felting makes an item shrink in size as the fibers lock together. It is important for the fiber to be a wool that has not been given superwash treatment. Superwash wools—and synthetic fibers—do not felt. Also, white or very light colors bleached by the manufacturer do not always felt as readily as darker colors. Because results can vary widely, it is a good idea to test felt with swatches first and take careful notes and measurements. Variables such as the yarn itself, different colors of the same yarn, water temperature, and soap can all affect the final product. Some yarns felt very quickly, others may require several machine cycles before they reach the desired stage.

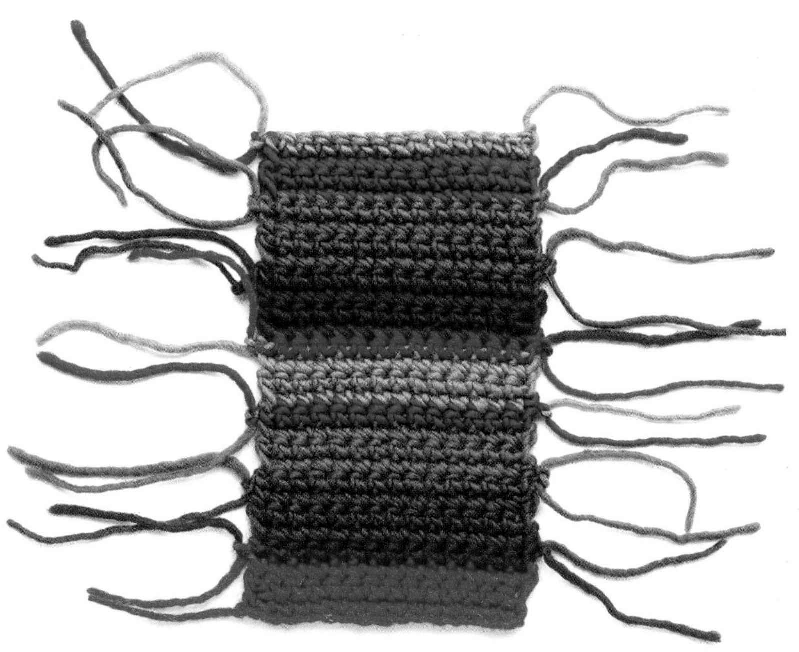

Swatch before felting

Felting occurs when the fiber is "shocked," a result achieved by agitation and contrasts in water temperature. Simple felting can be done in the washing machine with a hot wash and cold rinse in a regular cycle. Set the machine for a small load. Add a very small amount of mild detergent or dishwashing liquid. Too many suds can hamper the felting process, so use soap sparingly. Placing the item in a zippered pillow cover or zippered lingerie bag augments the agitation process (fibers rubbing against each other) and keeps loose fibers from clogging the washing machine. Put old towels (less lint) or T-shirts in the washing machine with the item being felted to improve agitation and keep the load balanced. Allow the item to go through the wash and rinse cycle, but, to keep it from becoming distorted, remove it before the spin process starts. If the felted item does not shrink sufficiently during the first wash cycle, don't drain the water from the machine; simply reset the wash cycle and allow the piece to go through again, testing frequently for shrinkage. Remember, it is almost impossible to stretch an over-felted piece to increase its size, so it is best to go slowly and check often until you obtain the desired size.

Remove excess water by wrapping the piece in several large bath towels and squeezing. Pull the item into shape, pat the edges smooth, and straighten any distortions by pulling and patting the piece into shape. Allow the piece to air dry. Felted items can be dried in the dyer, but the hot air may cause further shrinkage. Check felted machine drying frequently.

LESS IS MORE

BAGS

These little silk bags are fanciful and practical at the same time. They can be a wonderful container for a small special gift or a simple, handy solution as to where to keep your glasses or cell phone. Given their small size, they provide a format for sampling the technique of tapestry crochet.

SPECIFICATIONS

■ **SIZE**

Cosmetic Bag: 6" (15 cm) wide, 4½" (11.5 cm) long; Drawstring Bag: 3½" (9 cm) diameter (bottom), 5¾" (14.5 cm) long, 12¾" (32 cm) circumference at top opening; Neck Bag: 4" (10 cm) wide, 5¼" (13.5 cm) long, with 36" (91.5 cm) cord.

■ **YARN**

Fine-weight silk, about 300 yd (277 m) total. ***We used:*** Jaeger 4-ply Silk (100% pure silk; 201 yd [186 m] /50 g): 1 ball each #130 ivory (A), #131 silver blue (B), #136 midnight (C), #137 jet (D), # 138 tapestry (E). Cosmetic Bag: Colors B, C, D, E; Drawstring Bag: Colors A, B, C, D, E; Neck Bag: Colors B, C, D. **Note:** One ball of each color is sufficient for all three bags. Yardage is listed separately for each project, but don't increase yardage if making all three pieces.

■ **HOOK**

Size C/2 (2.75 mm) and D/3 (3.25 mm). Adjust hook size if necessary to obtain the correct gauge.

■ **NOTIONS**

Cosmetic Bag: Three buttons about ⅝" (1.5 cm) in diameter. Neck Bag: About 140 beads in size E, and two colors to coordinate with yarn colors—60 beads in dark color and 80 beads in light color; sharp sewing needle to use when attaching beads; T-pin or large safety pin for anchoring cord. For all bags: Contrasting lightweight yarn or safety pins for marking stitches, tapestry needle for working in yarn tails.

■ **GAUGE**

15 stitches and 16 rounds = 2" (5 cm) in circular single crochet with size D/3 (3.25 mm) hook.

■ **ABBREVIATIONS**

beg—beginning
ch(s)—chain(s)
lp(s)—loop(s)
rep—repeat
rnd(s)—round(s)
sc—single crochet
sk—skip
sl st—slip stitch
st(s)—stitch(es)

Review Basics, page 2
Chain stitch
Increasing
Reading a pattern
Single crochet
Weaving in ends

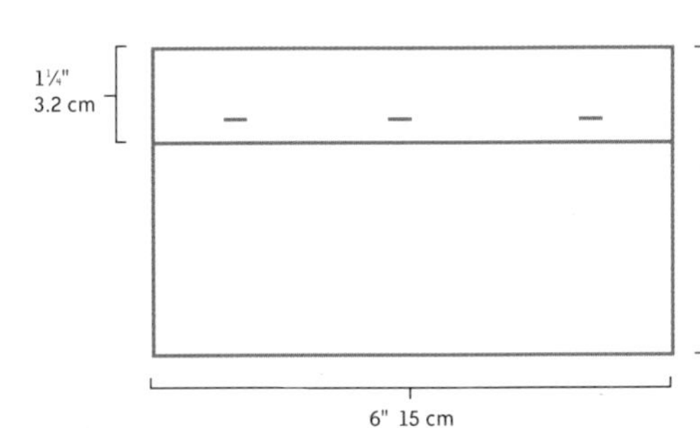

■ **COSMETIC BAG**

With size D/3 (3.25 mm) hook and color C, ch 49 sts. Beg in second ch from hook and work 1 sc in each of ch 47, end row with 2 sc in last ch. Do not turn work. Continuing around the opposite side of ch, work 1 sc in each of the next 47 chs—96 sts. Using either a small safety pin or contrasting thread woven in and out of one or two sts, mark both ends of the ch. Beg Chart I, working sc in Rnds 1–36 changing colors (see page 17) as shown, then working Rows 1–10 on half the number of sts to make the flap. Or, follow the text instructions as follows, working ch 1 at the beg of each rnd, then joining rnd (see page 23) with sl st in ch 1 at the end of each rnd.

TAPESTRY CROCHET

Single crochet provides a natural format for multicolor patterning in the reversible fabric known as tapestry crochet. This technique allows you to create simple geometric or pictoral designs. Normally, the designs are charted on graph paper, with each square representing a stitch and each line representing a row. The blank squares are the background color and the filled-in squares are the second color.

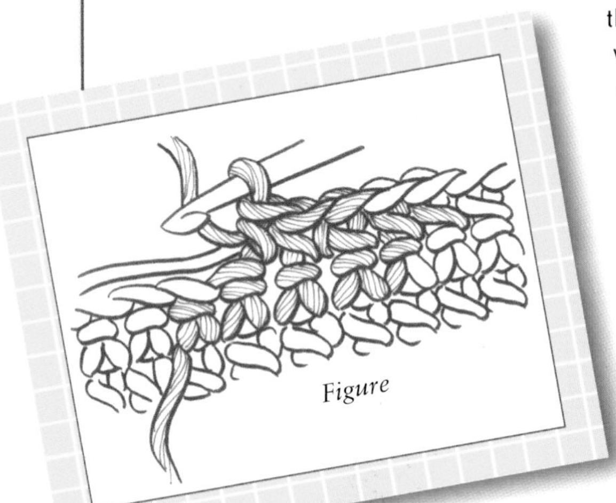
Figure

The method for crocheting with more than one color is as follows: Carry the second color inside the background color of the stitches being worked and change colors as needed. Simply lay the color not in use across the top of the stitches to be worked (Figure). When you want to change colors pull the new color to the back and into a working position around your finger and lay the old color forward across the top of the stitches. Avoid twisting the yarns. Don't work with more than two colors per row to avoid tangling and distorted row gauge.

To conceal the carried yarn, work tapestry crochet with a hook that's small in relation to yarn weight. Single crochet creates a dense fabric on its own, and the small hook and extra yarn that's carried along inside the stitch create an even denser fabric. Therefore, the technique is best used for items like bags and baskets. Tapestry crochet can be used in garments if the yarn is lightweight but it's best suited for coats and jackets.

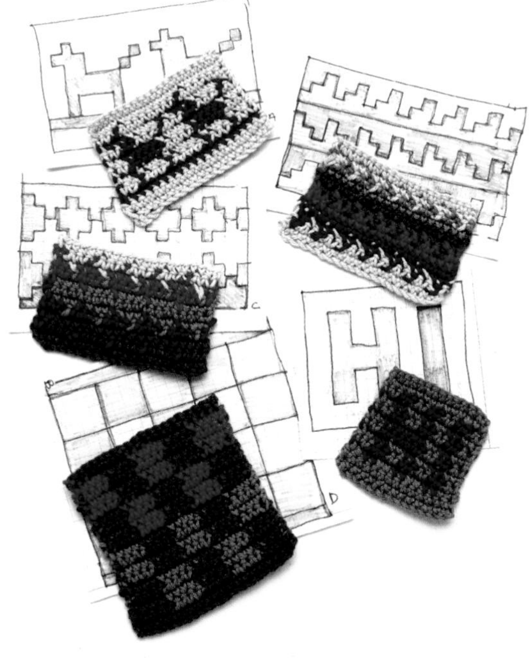

Tension can be tricky when you're working in tapestry crochet, especially with a slippery yarn like silk. Take care not to pull too tightly when you pick up a carried color, otherwise the previous stitch in that color can become very tight and difficult to work into on the next row or round. At the same time, a stitch that is too loose will distort a design. Even tension comes with practice.

Rnds 1–3: With color C, work 3 rnds in sc, keeping the side edges marked. Fasten off as follows: Cut yarn leaving 4" (10 cm) tail, insert tail through last lp on hook and pull to tighten.
Rnds 4–6: Attach color E and work in sc. Fasten off color E.
Rnds 7–8: Attach color B and work in sc. Fasten off color B.
Rnds 9–11: Attach color E and work in sc. Fasten off color E.
Rnds 12–15: Attach color C and work in sc. Fasten off color C.
Begin tapestry crochet: *Rnds 16–18:* Attach color E and work 4 sc, lay color E along the top of the sts in the row below, attach color B and work 4 sc, working over color E (see Tapestry Crochet, page 58). *Work 4 sts in color E while carrying color B across top of the sc sts of the rnd below, sc 4 sts in color B while carrying color E on top of the sc stitches of the rnd below*; rep from * to * around. Fasten off both colors.
Rnds 19–20: Attach color D, work in sc. Fasten off color D.
Rnds 21–23: Attach E and work 2 sc, lay color E along the top of the sts in the row below, attach color B, *work 4 sc each in color B and 4 sc in color E*; rep from * to * around, end with 2 sc in color E. Fasten off both colors.
Rnds 24–27: Attach color C and work in sc. Fasten off color C.
Rnds 28–30: Attach color E and work in sc. Fasten off color E.
Rnds 31–32: Attach color B and work in sc. Fasten off color B.
Rnds 33–35: Attach color E and work in sc. Fasten off color E.
Rnd 36: Attach color C and work in sc.

Flap: (worked flat, back and forth) With C, work the first 48 sts of next rnd. Turn, working on these 48 sts only, work 5 rows even. ***Buttonhole row*** (see page 71): On next row, ch 1, 5 sc, *ch 4, sk next 4 sts, work 1 sc in each of next 12 sc*, rep from * to * once more, ch 4, sk next 4 sts, work 1 sc in each of next 6 sc—3 buttonholes made. Continue in sc, working 1 sc in each st and each ch on the next row. Work 2 more rows even. Fasten off. With size C/2 (2.75 mm) hook attach color D at corner where the bag meets the flap. Work 1 rnd in reverse sc (see page 64) along the flap and the bag edges. Fasten off. Sew buttons on bag opposite buttonholes. Steam or block to size and shape.

DRAWSTRING BAG

With size D/3 (3.25 mm) hook and color E, ch 4 sts. Join with sl st to form ring (see page 23).
Rnd 1: Ch 3 (counts as 1 dc), work 11 dc into ring, join with sl st to top of ch 3—12 sts.
Rnd 2: Ch 1, work 2 sc in each dc, join with sl st to ch—24 sts.
Rnd 3: Ch 1, *work 1 sc in first sc, work 2 sc in next sc*; rep from * to * around, join with sl st to ch—36 sts.

Key for Small Bag Trio

- A #130 Ivory
- B #131 silver blue
- C #136 midnight
- D #137 jet
- E #138 tapestry
- work 1 sc using appropriate color as shown on chart
- pattern repeat frame
- 3 light-colored beads sewn to work when bag is finished. Refer to text for placement.
- 2 light-colored beads sewn to work when bag is finished. Refer to text for placement.
- 3 dark-colored beads sewn to work when bag is finished. Refer to text for placement.
- 2 dark-colored beads sewn to work when bag is finished. Refer to text for placement.

Chart I

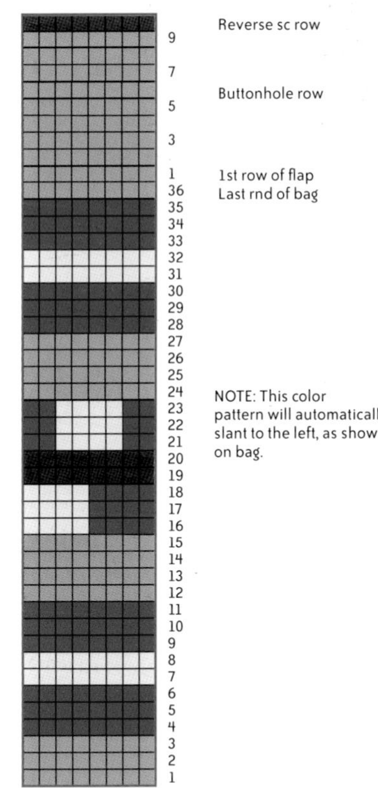

Rnds 1–36: Work color pattern over 96 sts.
Rows 1–9: Work color over 48 sts.
Final Trim: Work reverse sc as stated in text instructions.

Chart II

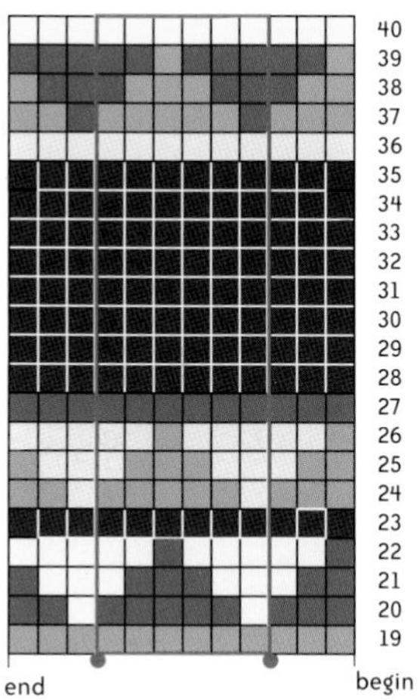

Work sts between markers 15 times.
NOTE: As each rnd is worked, the pattern automatically moves to the left and forms the triangular shapes as shown in photo.

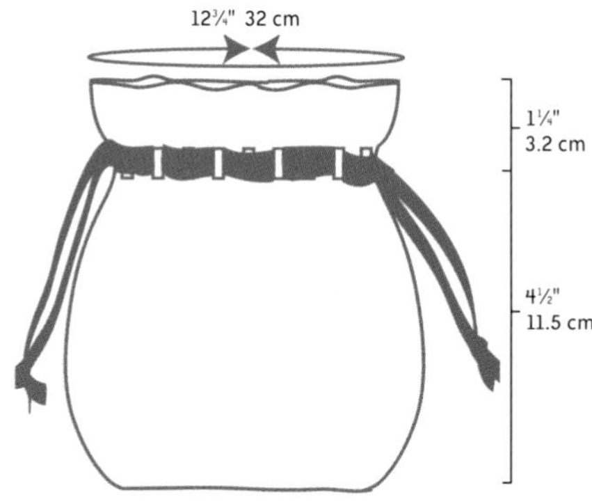

Rnd 4: Ch 1, *work 1 sc in each of first 2 sc, work 2 sc in next sc*; rep from * to * around, join with sl st to ch—48 sts.
Rnd 5: Ch 1, work even, join with sl st to ch.
Rnd 6: Ch 1, *work 1 sc in each of first 3 sc, work 2 sc in next sc*; rep from * to * around, join with sl st to ch—60 sts.
Rnd 7: Ch 1, work even, join to top of ch.
Rnd 8: Ch 1, *work 1 sc in each of first 4 sc, work 2 sc in next sc*; rep from * to * around, join with sl st to ch—72 sts.
Rnd 9: Ch 1, work even, join to top of ch. Fasten off color E.
Rnd 10: Attach color D. Ch 1, *work 1 sc in each of first 5 sc, work 2 sc in next sc*; rep from * to * around, join with sl st to ch—84 sts.
Rnd 11: Ch 1, work even, join with sl st to ch.
Rnd 12: Ch 1, *work 1 sc in each of first 6 sc, work 2 sc in next sc*; rep from * to * around, join with sl st to ch—96 sts.
Rnds 13–18: Continue with color D, ch 1, sc to end of rnd, join with sl st to ch. Fasten off color D.
Note: Follow Chart II for the Triangle Patterns, working Rnds 19 through 40 in colors as shown on chart. After Rnd 40, follow the instructions below.
Rnds 41–46: Attach color D and work in sc.
Rnd 47: (Eyelet Rnd) Ch 5, sk 2 sc, work 1 dc in third sc, *ch 2, sk 2 sc, work 1 dc in next sc*, rep from * to * to end of rnd. Join with sl st to third ch of ch 5.
Rnd 48: Ch 1, *work 2 sc in ch 2-sp, work 1 sc in dc*; rep from * to * around, join with sl st to ch.
Rnd 49: Ch 1, sc to end of rnd. Drop color D but do not fasten off.
Rnd 50: Attach color C, ch 1, and sc to end of rnd. Fasten off.
Rnd 51: With color D, ch 1, sc to end of rnd. Drop D but do not fasten off.
Rnd 52: Attach color E and work 1 rnd sc. Fasten off.
Rnds 53–54: Pick up color D and work 2 more rnds in sc.
Change to size C/2 (2.75 mm) hook and work 1 rnd reverse sc (see page 64). Fasten off.
Drawstring: (make 2) With size D/3 hook and two strands of color D held together, ch 100. Fasten off. Starting at beg of rnd, thread one drawstring weaving in and out through the eyelets. Thread second drawstring through eyelets beg at the opposite "side," and sharing eyelets. Knot ends of drawstring together 1" (2.5 cm) from end. Trim drawstring ends to create a short fringe trim.

NECK BAG

With size D/3 (3.25 mm) hook and color B, ch 29 sts. Work 1 sc in second ch from hook, then work 1 sc in each of next 26 ch. Work 2 sc in end ch. *Do not turn work*. Continuing around to the opposite edge of ch work 1 sc in next 27 ch for a total of 56 sts.
Rnds 1–9: With color B, ch 1, work 1 sc in each sc. Join each rnd with sl st to ch. Follow Chart III for pattern, working Rnds 10 through 40 in colors as shown.
Rnd 41: With color D, change to size C/2 (2.75 mm) hook and work 1 rnd reverse sc (see page 64). Fasten off all colors.

FINISHING

Cut a length of matching yarn about 18" (46 cm) long. Separate yarn plies and using one or two of the plies, sew beads at the ends of the tapestry "branches" (see Chart III)—two dark beads at each point of color D on the middle stripe and three beads at each point on top edge. Sew three lighter beads at each point on stripes of color C on front side of bag and two beads each at each point of color C stripes on the back of bag.

Strap: 36" 91.5 cm including side edges.

5½" 12.5 cm

3¾" 9.5 cm

TWISTED CORD STRAP

Cut two pieces of color D each 5 yd (4.57 m) long to make a 36" (91.5 cm) cord (or five times the desired length of finished cord). Holding two lengths together, fold strands in half and knot end. Fasten knot securely to a stationary point (you can stick a T-pin through the edge of a cushion). Twist cord tightly in one direction until entire cord is well twisted. Holding on to end, pinch cord in middle and fold it to meet the knotted end. Let go of the pinch and allow the cord to twist back on itself. Smooth out as necessary to even the twist and knot the ends about 1" (2.5 cm) from end.

Separate plies of silk to use as sewing thread, and with threaded sewing needle, attach cord to each side of bag, aligning the knots with the bottom of the bag on each side. Trim cord below the knot to create a small fringe.

Chart III

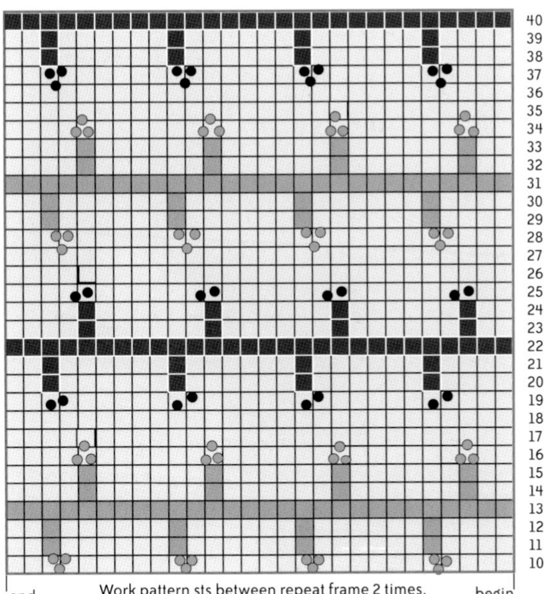

Bead placement simulated here is for the front of bag. Follow text instructions for bead placement on the back of bag.

Note: In tapestry crochet, the color pattern shifts to the left, and will appear same on bag.

TIMELESS

TANK TOP

Sleek and chic, this simple style transcends time with a ribbon yarn and an easy elongated stitch that shows off the yarn. Reverse crochet elegantly trims the edges.

SIZE

To fit 33 (37, 41, 45)" (84 [94, 104, 114.5] cm) bust circumference. Actual measurements 35 (39, 43, 47)" (89 [99, 109, 119.5] cm) bust circumference; 22 (23, 25, 26)" (56 [58.5, 63, 66] cm) length. Sweater shown measures 39"(99 cm).

YARN

Ribbon or light bulky yarn, about 550 (660, 660, 770) yd (503 [604, 604, 704] m).
We used: Berroco Zen (40% cotton, 60% nylon; 110 yd [102 m]/50 g): 5 (6, 6, 7) skeins #8244 umeboshi plum.

HOOK

Size H/8 (5 mm) and J/9 (6 mm). Adjust hook size if necessary to obtain the correct gauge.

GAUGE

13 stitches and 7 rows = 4" (10 cm) in double crochet with size J/9 (6 mm) hook.

ABBREVIATIONS

beg—begin(s), beginning
ch(s)—chain(s)
dc—double crochet
lp(s)—loop(s)
rep—repeat
sc—single crochet
sk—skip
sl st—slip stitch
st(s)—stitches

Review Basics, page 2:
Chain stitch
Decreasing
Double crochet
Reading a pattern
Seaming
Single crochet
Slip stitch
Weaving in ends

BACK

With larger size hook and yarn, loosely ch 58 (65, 71, 77) sts.
Row 1: Beg in second ch from hook, work 1 row sc—57 (64, 70, 76) sts. Turn work.
Row 2: Ch 3 (counts as 1 dc), sk the first sc st at side edge, work 1 dc in each sc st to end of row.
Row 3: Ch 3 (counts as 1 dc), sk first dc at side edge, work 1 dc in each st across row—57 (64, 70, 76) sts. Rep Row 3 until back measures 14 (15, 16, 17)" (35.5 [38, 40.5, 43] cm) from beg of work.

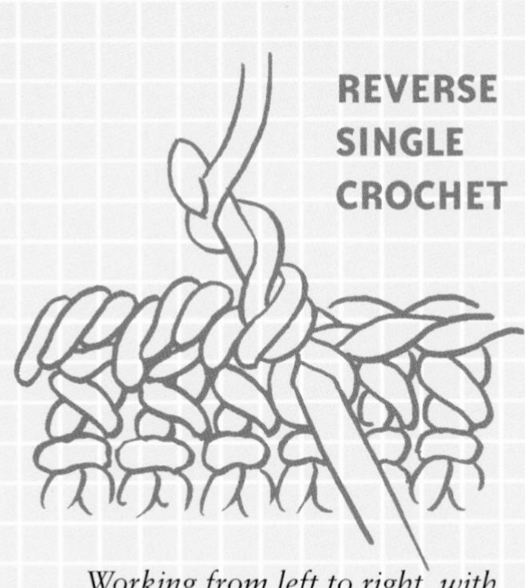

Working from left to right, with right-side facing, chain one. Single crochet in stitch nearest the hook.

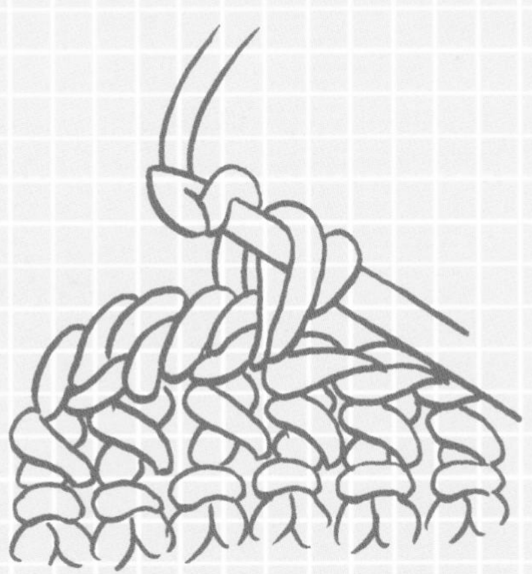

Bring yarn through both loops on hook. Single crochet across the row from left to right.

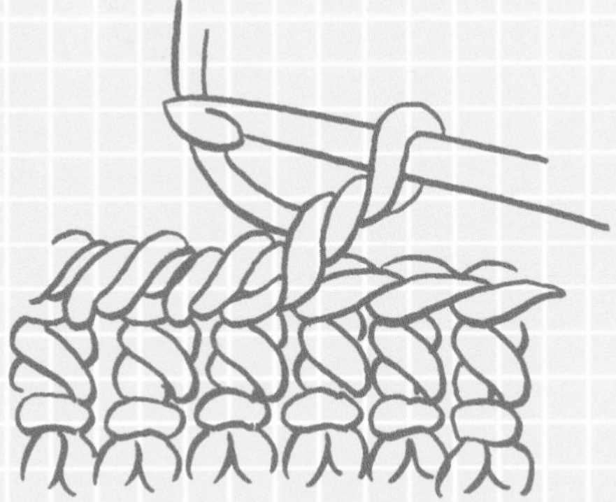

*Chain 1, * skip 1, reverse single crochet in next stitch, * repeat from * to *.*

SHAPE ARMHOLE

On next row, omitting ch 3 after turning, work sl st in first 3 sts, ch 3 in next dc (counts as 1 dc), then work 1 dc in each of next 50 (57, 63, 69) dc—51 (58, 64, 70) sts remain. Turn work. On next row, omitting ch 3 after turning, sl st in first 2 sts, ch 3 in next dc (counts as 1 dc), work dc in each of next 46 (53, 59, 65) dc—47 (54, 60, 66) sts remain. *Turn. On next row sl st in first st, ch 3 in next dc (counts as 1 dc), work 1 dc in each st until 1 st remains, sk that dc*. Rep from * to * 4 (4, 6, 6) more times—a total of 37 (44, 46, 52) sts remain. Work even until armhole measures 4 (4, 5, 5)" (10 [10, 12.5, 12.5] cm).

SHAPE NECK

Row 1: Ch 3 (counts as 1 dc), sk first dc at side edge, work across 15 (18, 18, 21) dc—16 (19, 19, 22) sts remain.
Row 2: Turn, sl st in first 2 sts, ch 3 in next dc (counts as 1 dc), work 1 dc in each dc to end of row (2 decreases made)—14 (17, 17, 20) sts remain.
Row 3: Turn, ch 3 (counts as 1 dc), sk first dc at side edge, work 1 dc in each of next 11 (14, 14, 17) dc sts (2 decreases made)—12 (15, 15, 18) sts remain.
Row 4: Turn, sl st in first 2 dc, ch 3 in next dc (counts as first dc), work 1 dc in each of next 9 (12, 12, 15) dc sts (2 decreases made)—10 (13, 13, 16) sts remain.
Row 5: Turn, ch 3 (counts as 1 dc), sk first dc, work 1 dc in each of next 8 (11, 11, 14) dc sts (1 decrease made)—9 (12, 12, 15) sts remain.
Row 6: Turn, sl st in first dc, ch 3 in next dc (counts as 1 dc), work 1 dc in each of next 7 (10, 10, 13) dc sts (1 decrease made)—8 (11, 11, 14) sts remain.
Row 7: Turn, ch 3 (counts as 1 dc), sk first dc, work 1 sc in each of next 7 (9, 9, 12) dc (1 decrease made on each of last 3 sizes only)—8 (10, 10, 13) sts remain.
Work even on 8 (10, 10, 13) sts until armhole measures 8 (8, 9, 9)" (20.5 [20.5, 23, 23] cm). Fasten off as follows: Cut yarn leaving 4" (10 cm) tail, insert tail through last stitch on hook and pull to tighten and secure. Attach yarn at opposite edge and work shaping of second shoulder to correspond to first.

FRONT

Work same as Back.

FINISHING

Work in loose ends to wrong side of work. With right sides together, sl st crochet shoulder seams. Sl st crochet side seams, leaving a 3" (7.5 cm) opening at lower edge.

Armhole edges: With smaller size crochet hook and right side of work facing, join yarn at underarm seam. Work 60 (66, 66, 72) sc evenly spaced around armhole edge, join with sl st. Ch 1, work 1 reverse sc (see page 64) in each sc. Fasten off.

Neck edge: With smaller size crochet hook and right side of work facing, join yarn at shoulder seam. Work 78 (84, 84, 90) sc evenly spaced around neck edge. Join with sl st. Ch 1, work 1 reverse sc in each sc. Fasten off.

Lower edge: With smaller size crochet hook and right side of work facing, join yarn at side seam. Work 9 sc evenly spaced along vent, 2 sc in corner, 55 (62, 68, 74) sc along lower edge, 2 sc in corner, 9 sc spaced along vent, 1 sc at side seam, 9 sc along vent, 2 sc in corner st, 55 (62, 68, 74) sc along lower edge, 2 sc in corner st, 9 sc spaced along vent, 1 sc at side seam. Join with sl st. Work 1 reverse sc in each sc. Fasten off.

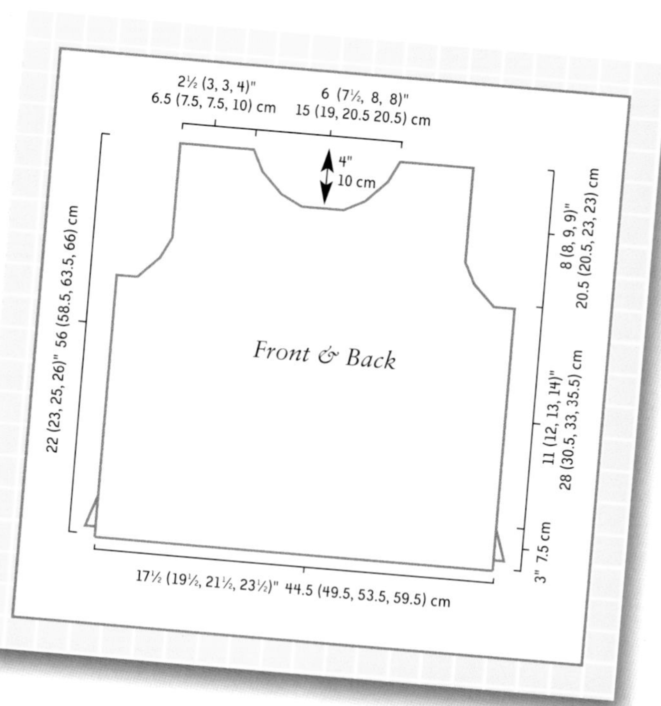

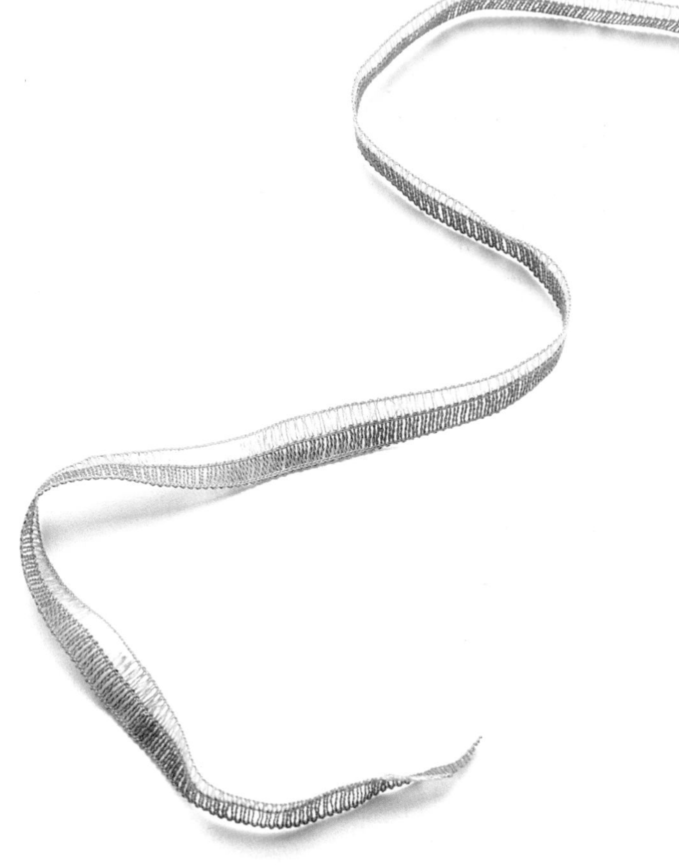

STITCHED TO

SUIT

EASY SKIRT

Mini or maxi, you choose what's right for the occasion and make it to suit. Even though the mini version is shown here, you can lengthen it easily by working more rows. Tight elastic lets it be worn at the natural waist while loose elastic lets it ride hip-top. For those who prefer an overall loose fit, make the skirt a size larger and adjust the elastic.

S P E C I F I C A T I O N S

SIZE

To fit size S (M, L, XL); 36 (40, 44, 48)" (91.5 [101.5, 112, 122] cm) hip circumference; 18 (18, 19, 19)" (46 [46, 48.5, 48.5] cm) length.

YARN

Sportweight yarn, about 1000 (1100, 1200, 1300) yd [923 (1015, 1108, 1200) m]. ***We used:*** Louet Gems Sportweight Merino (100% merino wool;198 yd [181 m]/ 100 g): 6 (6, 7, 8) skeins, #02 tobacco.

HOOK

Size E/4 (3.5 mm). Adjust hook size if necessary to obtain the correct gauge.

NOTIONS

Elastic ¾" (2 cm) wide, comfortable waist measurement plus 2" (5 cm) long; tapestry needle; sewing needle, sewing thread to coordinate with elastic color; safety pins or long sewing pins with large colored heads.

GAUGE

20 stitches and 14 rounds = 4" (10 cm) worked in circular pattern stitch on size E/4 (3.5 mm) crochet hook.

ABBREVIATIONS

beg—beginning
ch—chain
dc—double crochet
inc—increase
lp(s)—loop(s)
rep—repeat
rnd(s)—round(s)
sc—single crochet
sk—skip
sl st—slip stitch
st(s)—stitch(es)

Review Basics, page 2:
Chain stitch
Double crochet
Increasing
Reading a pattern
Seaming
Single crochet
Slip stitch
Weaving in ends
Working in rounds

PATTERN STITCH

Circular Pattern Stitch: Worked over an even number of stitches
Chain an even number of stitches. Join rnd with sl st (see page 23).
Rnd 1: Ch 1, work 1 sc in each ch. Join rnd with sl st.
Rnd 2: Ch 3 (counts as 1 dc), work 1 dc in same st as ch 3, sk next st, *work 2 dc in next st, sk next st*; rep from * to * around. Join rnd with sl st to top of ch 3.
Rep Rnds 1 and 2 for pattern st.

CHOOSING BUTTONS

Choosing just the right button is a great way to individualize a cardigan. This is one detail where mass manufacturers often cut corners, but when you are creating a one-of-a-kind garment you have the luxury of splurging on a really effective button. Even when it's desirable to have the buttons blend into the sweater, quality natural materials such as shell, wood, or bone add a touch of elegance.

When you're choosing buttons, there are just a few factors to consider. The first is weight. A heavy button will eventually stretch the button side of your cardigan so that the fronts will be two different lengths when it's worn open. Stretching can be remedied in most cases by reinforcing the buttonband, usually by sewing a ribbon behind it. For a rolled-edge sweater with no formal band it is best to choose a lightweight button. The second factor to consider is shape. An oddly shaped button requires a large buttonhole. The third factor to consider is compatibility of care. If your sweater is washable and the buttons are not, you may have to remove and replace them every time you launder your sweater. Keeping these considerations in mind, have fun choosing buttons.

SKIRT

(worked in one piece)
With hook and yarn, loosely ch 180 (200, 220, 240) sts. Join with sl st to form rnd.

Lower border pattern:

Rnd 1: Ch 1, work 1 sc in each ch, join rnd with sl st to top of ch 1 (see page 23).

Rnds 2 and 3: Ch1, work 1 sc in each sc, join rnd with sl st to top of ch 1.

Change to main Circular Pattern Stitch, beg with Rnd 1 work until skirt measures a total length of 17 (17, 18, 18)" (43 [43, 46, 46] cm), ending with Rnd 2. ***Casing:*** Work 2" (5 cm) in sc, beg each rnd with ch 1, and join the rnd end with a sl st. Fasten off as follows: Cut yarn leaving 4" (10 cm) tail, insert tail through last lp to hook and pull to tighten.

FINISHING

Place joining point of rounds at center back. Fold the upper edge of the single crochet section in half to the inside to form a waistband casing; pin in place. With yarn threaded on tapestry needle, whipstitch casing in place, leaving a 3" (7.5 cm) opening at the center back. Remove pins. Cut elastic to a comfortable waist measurement plus 2" (5 cm) for overlap. Insert a large safety pin through one end of the elastic, and thread elastic through casing. Remove safety pin. Join elastic ends together securely by lapping one end over the other. Keep the join as flat as possible while working, and don't allow the elastic to twist before sewing the join. Using sewing thread and needle, backstitch around the overlap edges. With yarn threaded on tapestry needle, whipstitch waistband opening closed. Weave in all loose ends to wrong side of skirt and secure. Block or steam skirt as needed.

Have fun with your button choice

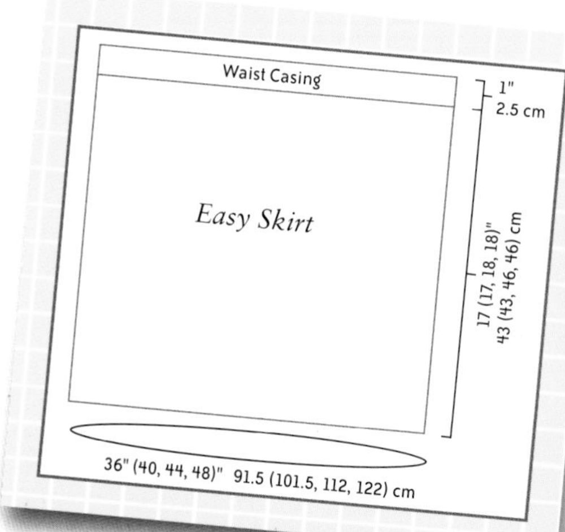

SPECIFICATIONS

SIZE

S (M, L, XL); 40 (44, 48, 52)" (101.5 [112, 122, 132] cm) bust/chest circumference; 21 (22, 23, 24)" (53.5 [56, 58.5. 61] cm) length. Sweater shown measures 44" (112 cm).

YARN

Sportweight yarn, about 1700 (1800, 1900, 2000) yd (1555 [1646, 1737, 1829] m). ***We used:*** Louet Gems Sportweight Merino (100% merino wool; 198 yd [181 m] meters]/100 g]); #02 tobacco, 9 (10, 10, 11) skeins.

HOOK

Size E/4 (3.5 mm). Adjust hook size if necessary to obtain the correct gauge.

NOTIONS

Five buttons, ¾" (2 cm) in diameter; tapestry needle; safety pins; *optional* sewing needle and thread to attach buttons.

GAUGE

22 stitches and 14 rows = 4" (10 cm) in pattern stitch with size E/4 (3.5 mm) hook.

This classic V-neck cardigan is boxy and loose fitting. The pockets are optional—perfectly functional on a jacket sweater, but you may want to eliminate them for a dressy look. Emphasize the boxy style by crocheting the cardigan short or make it long to wear over everything.

EASY CARDIGAN

ABBREVIATIONS

beg—begin(s), beginning
ch—chain
dc—double crochet
est—establish(ed)
inc—increase(s)
patt—pattern(s)
rep—repeat
sc—single crochet
sk—skip
sl st—slip stitch
st(s)—stitch(es)

Review Basics, page 2:
Buttonholes
Chain stitch
Decreasing
Double crochet
Increasing
Reading a pattern
Single crochet
Slip stitch
Weaving in ends

PATTERN STITCH

Worked over an even number of stitches
Row 1: Work 1 sc in each st. Turn work.
Row 2: Ch 3 (counts as 1 dc), sk first sc, *work 2 dc in next sc, sk next sc*; rep from * to * to last sc, work 1 dc in last sc. Ch 1, turn work.
Rep Rows 1 and 2 for patt.

Easy Cardigan

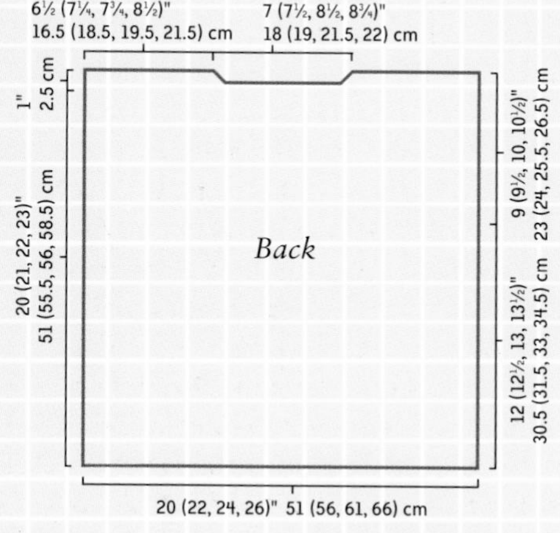

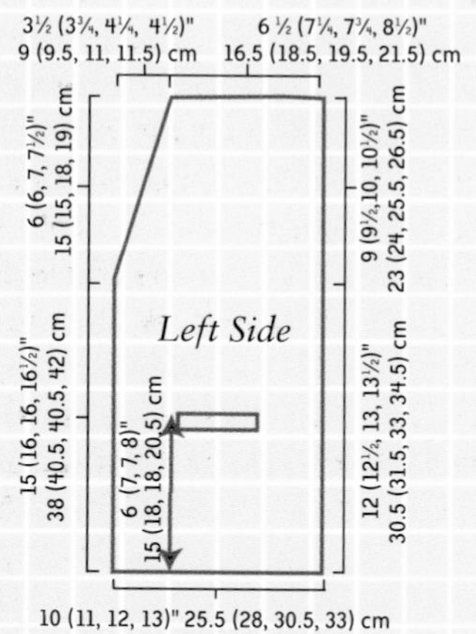

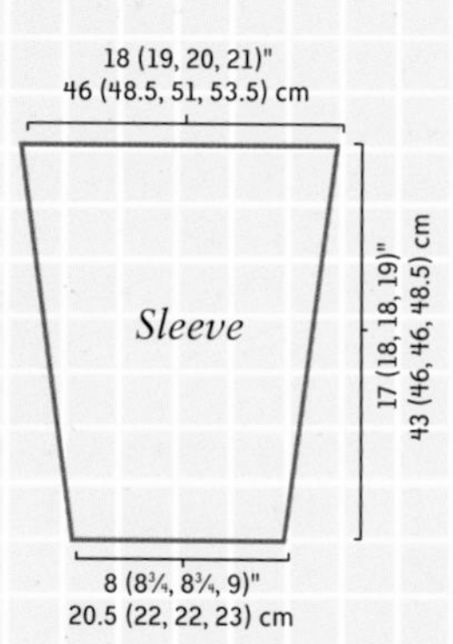

BACK

With hook and yarn , ch 111 (121,133,145) sts.
Row 1: Sc 110 (120, 132, 144) sts. Turn.
Rows 2–3: Ch 1 (for height, does not count as st), sc 110 (120, 132, 144 sts). Turn.
Ch 1 and beg patt st with Row 1 (RS). Work in patt st until back measures a total length of 20 (21, 22, 23)" (51 [53.5, 56, 58.5] cm) ending with a Row 2. ***Shape back neck:*** Work each side separately, beg at right shoulder.
Next row: (RS) Work across 39 (42, 46, 50) sts in est patt. Turn.
Next row: Sl st across first 3 sts at neck edge, ch 3, cont in patt across 36 (39, 43, 47) sts. Work even in est patt on 36 (39, 43, 47) sts until back measures a total length of 21 (22, 23, 24)" (53.5 [56, 58.5, 61] cm). Fasten off as follows: Cut yarn leaving a 4" (10 cm) tail, insert tail through last st on hook and pull to tighten and secure.
Left side of neck: (WS) Attach yarn at 71 (78, 86, 94) st counting across from the right side edge of back, sl st across first 3 sts at neckline edge, ch 3, cont in est patt to end of row, turn.
Next row: Work in est patt over next 36 (39, 43, 47) sts. Continue working left side of neck and shoulder in est patt on 36 (39, 43, 47 sts). When work measures 21 (22, 23, 24)" (53.5 [56, 58.5. 61] cm), end with Row 2 and fasten off.

LEFT FRONT

With hook and yarn, ch 55, (61, 67, 73) sts. Work 3 rows sc on 54 (60, 66, 72) sts. Change to patt st beg with Row 1 and work even until front measures 6 (7, 7, 8)" (15 [18, 18, 20.5] cm) from beg, ending with a Row 2. ***Pocket opening:*** Work across the first 9 (12, 15, 18) sts, ch 36, sk next 36 sts, work in est patt across rem 9 (12, 15, 18) sts. Cont in patt working into chain 36 on the next row. Work even in patt until front measures a total length of 15 (16, 16, 16½)" (38 [40.5, 40.5, 42] cm) from the beg, ending with Row 2. **Note:** The following neck shaping decreases are worked as follows: Work to 1 st from the end of row when decrease is at end of row, or work a sl st over first st at the beg of row. ***Shape Neck:*** (RS) Decrease 1 st at the end of the next row, *and at same edge* every row 17 (20, 22, 24) more times. Work even on 36 (39, 43, 47) sts until the front is same length as back. Fasten off.

RIGHT FRONT

Work same as Left Front, reversing neck shaping.

SLEEVES

(Make 2)
With hook and yarn, ch 45 (49, 49, 51) sts. Work 3 rows sc on 44

(48, 48, 50) sts. Change to patt st, beg with Row 1. Work 2 rows even. **Note:** In the following sleeve increase, work an extra sc at each side when inc occur in Row 1, and an extra dc at each side when inc occur on Row 2. Cont in patt st, inc 1 st each side edge in the next row, and then every other row for a total of 26 (28, 31, 33) times—96 (104, 110, 115) sts. When sleeve measures 17 (18, 18, 19)" (43 [46, 46, 48.5] cm) work 1 row of sc. Fasten off.

FINISHING

With right sides together, slip-stitch crochet shoulders together. Mark the center top of sleeve with a safety pin. Measure down 9 (9½, 10, 10½)" (23 [24, 25.5, 26.5] cm) from the shoulder seam on both front and back of body, and place a safety pin to mark each side. These pins mark the armhole opening. With right sides of work together, align the sleeve top edge pin with the shoulder seam, and smooth the sleeve top out between the two safety pins marking the armhole (see Setting a Sleeve into an Armhole, page 74). Pin the sleeve in place and attach sleeve to armhole with slip-stitch crochet. Then slip-stitch crochet the side and sleeve seams in one, leaving the sc edges open both at the bottom edge and sleeve bottom. Remove all pins. Weave in all ends to wrong side of work and secure.

Pocket Lining: With RS facing, attach yarn at the upper edge of pocket opening. Work 1 sc in each ch (the 36 chs that formed the pocket opening), turn. Ch 3, (counts as 1 dc) work in dc until lining measures a total length of 5" (12.5 cm). Fasten off. Pin lining to front. Thread tapestry needle with yarn and whipstitch lining in place on the inside of front. Remove pins.

Pocket Trim: With RS facing, attach yarn at the top edge of pocket. Work sc over next 36 pocket sts. Work 2 more rows sc. Fasten off. With threaded tapestry needle, tack the side edges of the pocket trim in place on the front.

Front Band: With RS of work facing, beg at lower edge work about 264 (276, 296, 308) sc evenly around front and neck edge. Adjust the numbers if necessary. The band should lie smoothly and evenly along the fronts, and is slightly eased around the back neck. Work 3 more rows in sc working five 2-st buttonholes evenly along right-front edge, placing the top buttonhole ½" (1.3 cm) below point of the V-neck and the bottom buttonhole 1" (2.5 cm) above lower edge. Space the other 3 buttonholes evenly between, about every 2¾, (3, 3, 3½)" (7 [7.5, 7.5, 9] cm) if buttons and buttonholes are the same size. With yarn, or sewing thread to match yarn color, sew buttons in place opposite buttonholes. Steam or block as needed.

BUTTONHOLES

Buttonholes are very easily and neatly worked in crochet. The most stable buttonhole is worked in single crochet as it's the least likely to stretch.

The first step in making a buttonhole is to determine placement and size. Often a pattern will only state the number of buttonholes needed and the space in which they are to be worked. For a very small button, one stitch is all that is necessary, but in most cases, the average button (¾–1¼" [2–3.2 cm] in diameter) will require a two- or three-stitch buttonhole. Buttonholes will stretch a little with use so plan on a snug fit at first, but make sure the button can fit through the opening. Multiply the number of buttonholes required by the number of stitches in each buttonhole. Subtract this number from the total number of stitches (rows) in the buttonhole band. Divide the remaining stitches evenly to be worked between the buttonholes as well as above the top buttonhole and below the bottom buttonhole. Sometimes it is helpful to draw out a chart that plots buttonhole placement.

To make a horizontal buttonhole, follow pattern directions until you're at the designated place for the first buttonhole. Work as follows: *chain the number of stitches needed, skip the corresponding number of stitches on the band (Figure 1), and then resume working single crochet to the next buttonhole placement** and repeat from * to ** until all buttonholes are completed. On the next row, work a single crochet stitch in each of the chain stitches (Figure 2). To further reinforce a buttonhole opening, work a buttonhole (embroidery) stitch around the opening after finishing.

Figure 1

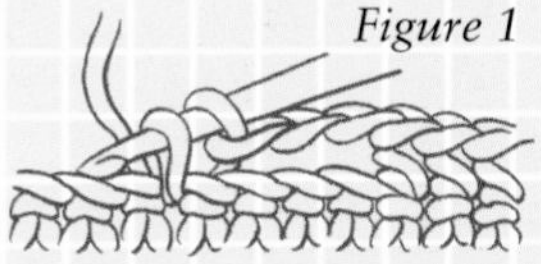

Figure 2

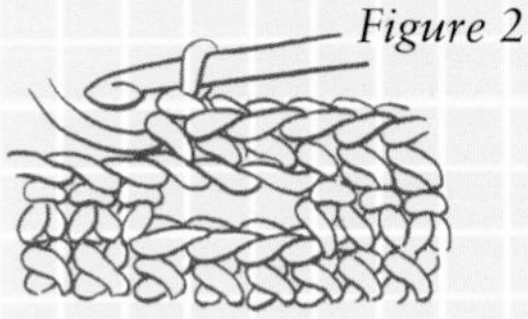

SPECIFICATIONS

SIZE

To fit size S (M, L, XL); 38 (42, 46, 50)" (95 [105, 115, 125] cm bust/chest circumference. Sweater shown measures 42" (105 cm).

YARN

Sportweight yarn, about 1600 (1750, 1800, 1900) yd (1475 [1615, 1660, 1750] m). ***We used:*** Louet Gems Sportweight Merino (100% merino wool; 198 yd [181 m]/100 g): 8 (9, 9, 10) skeins, # 35 mustard.

HOOK

Size E/4 (3.5 mm). Adjust hook size if necessary to obtain the correct gauge.

NOTIONS

Safety pins, or long sewing pins with large heads; tapestry needle.

GAUGE

20 stitches and 14 rows = 4" (10 cm) in pattern stitch with size E/4 (3.5 mm) hook.

This is a perfect first sweater because the pattern stitch is easy and creates an interesting texture. The funnel neck and dropped shoulders call for a minimum of shaping yet still present a fashionable silhouette. Make the pullover oversized but short to leave room for layering or fit it close for a classic look.

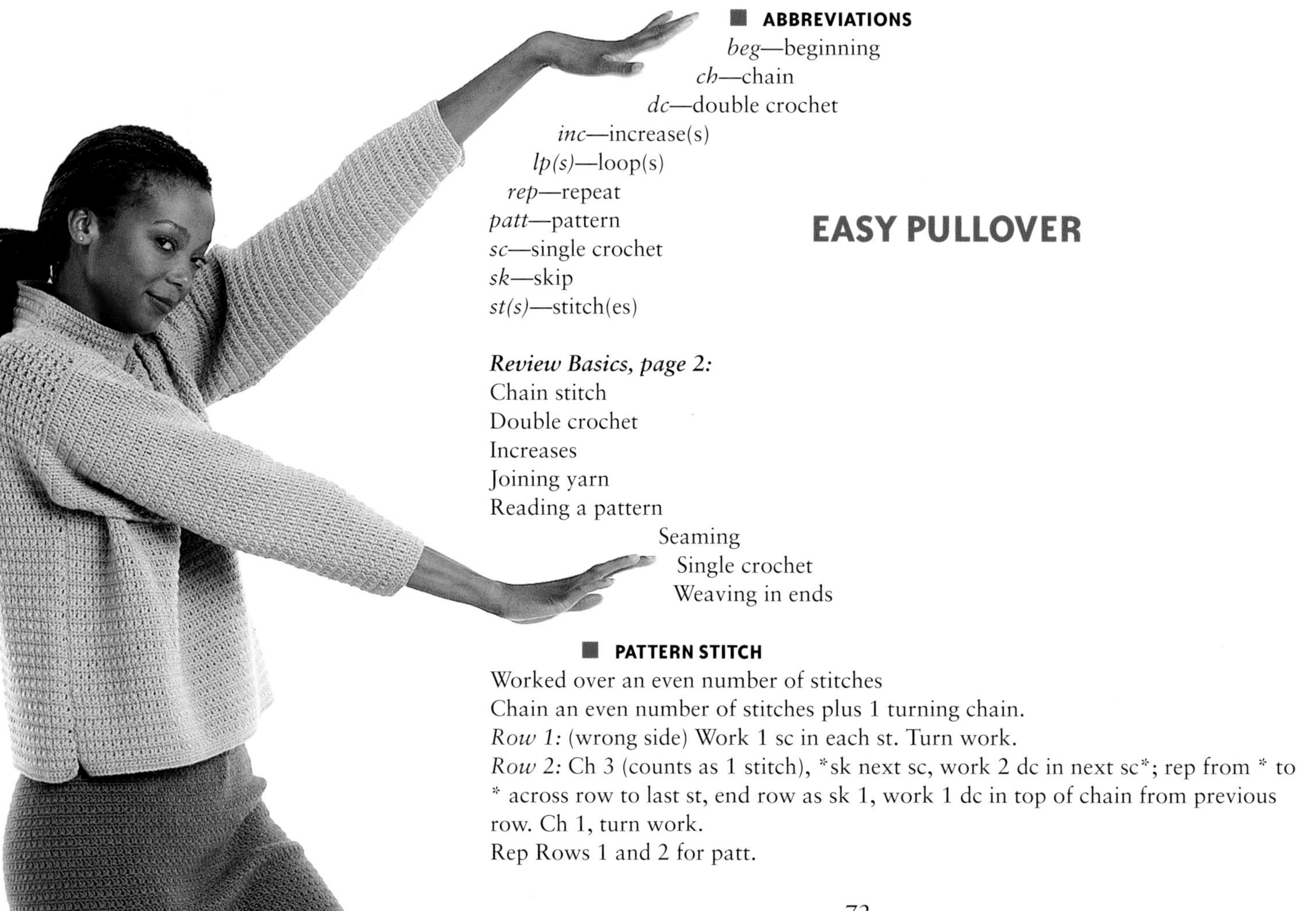

EASY PULLOVER

ABBREVIATIONS

beg—beginning
ch—chain
dc—double crochet
inc—increase(s)
lp(s)—loop(s)
rep—repeat
patt—pattern
sc—single crochet
sk—skip
st(s)—stitch(es)

Review Basics, page 2:
Chain stitch
Double crochet
Increases
Joining yarn
Reading a pattern
Seaming
Single crochet
Weaving in ends

PATTERN STITCH

Worked over an even number of stitches
Chain an even number of stitches plus 1 turning chain.
Row 1: (wrong side) Work 1 sc in each st. Turn work.
Row 2: Ch 3 (counts as 1 stitch), *sk next sc, work 2 dc in next sc*; rep from * to * across row to last st, end row as sk 1, work 1 dc in top of chain from previous row. Ch 1, turn work.
Rep Rows 1 and 2 for patt.

BACK

With hook and yarn, loosely ch 97 (107, 117, 127) sts. ***Lower border:*** *Sc 96 (106, 116, 126), turn. Ch 1*. Rep from * to * for 2 more rows (3 sc rows). Change to main patt st and beg with Row 1 (wrong side), work in patt until piece measures 21 (22, 23, 24)" (53.5 [56, 58.5, 61] cm) from beg ch, ending with a Row 1. Fasten off as follows: Cut yarn leaving 4" (10 cm) tail, insert tail through last lp on hook and pull to tighten and secure.

Funnel Neck: With right side of work facing, attach yarn at stitch 26 (32, 34, 39) from right-hand edge. Ch 3 (counts as 1 st), starting with Row 2 of patt and following sts as established, work in patt st over next 44 (44, 50, 50) sts for a total length of 1¾" (4.3 cm). Work 3 rows sc. Fasten off.

5 (6, 6½, 7½)" 12.5 (15, 16.5, 19) cm
9 (9, 10, 10)" 23 (23, 25.5, 25.5) cm
2" 5 cm
21 (22, 23, 24)" 53.5 (56, 58.5, 61) cm
5" 12.5 cm
Pocket
5" 12.5 cm
Front & Back
9½ (10, 10, 10½)" 24 (25.5, 25.5, 26.5) cm
11½ (12, 13, 13½)" 29 (30.5, 33, 34.5) cm
19 (21, 23, 25)" 48.5 (53.5, 58.5, 63.5) cm

FRONT

Work same as Back.

SLEEVES

(Make 2) With hook and yarn, loosely ch 45 (49, 49, 55) sts. *Sc 44 (48, 48, 54) sts, turn. Ch 1*. Rep from * to * for 2 more rows (3 sc rows). Change to patt st and beg with Row 1 (wrong side of work) work 2 rows even. Inc 1 st each end at beg of next row and then on every other row 23 more times for a total of 92 (96, 96, 102) sts. Work in patt without further inc until total sleeve length measures 17 (18, 18, 19)" (43 [46, 46, 48.5] cm), ending with a Row 1. Fasten off.

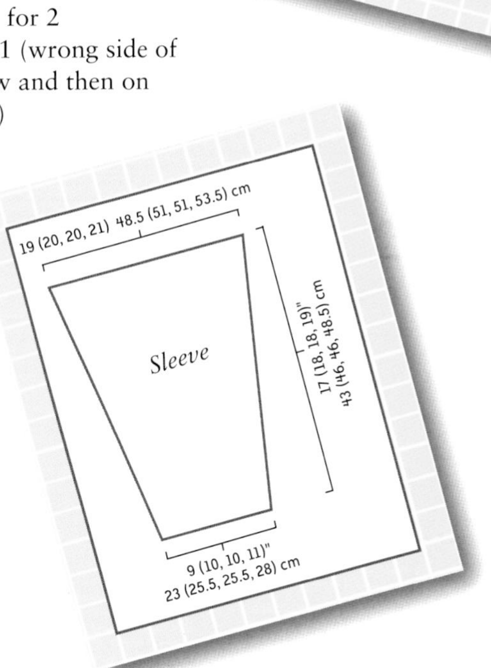

SEWING ON A BUTTON

If you're crocheting with a plied yarn, you can sew your buttons on with one of the plies or you can use a matching sewing thread doubled. Using a blunt-end needle that will fit through the hole in the button, insert the needle from the wrong side of the crocheted fabric into the button leaving about ¼" (6 mm) between the button and the crocheted fabric (Figure 1).

Take the needle through the next hole in the button and back into the fabric. Repeat this step as many times as you have buttonholes; end on the right side of the garment but under the button. To finish off, wrap your yarn or thread three to five times under the button and pull the yarn or thread through the thickness and back to the wrong side of the crocheted fabric (Figure 2). Fasten off.

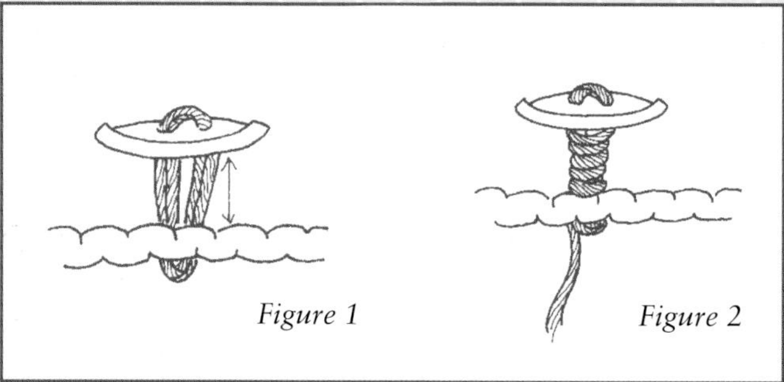

Figure 1 *Figure 2*

SETTING A SLEEVE INTO AN ARMHOLE

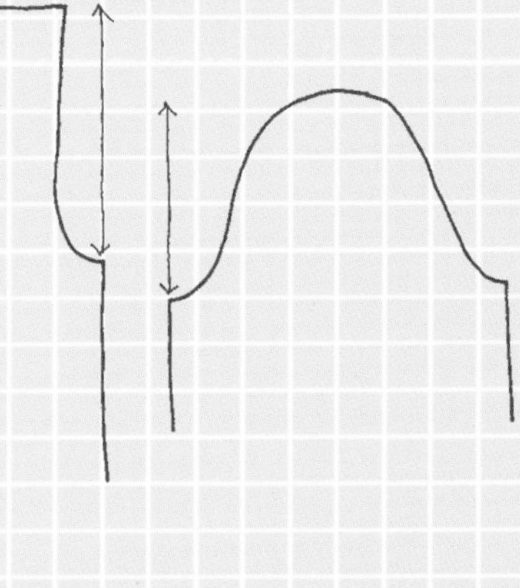

A garment with a set-in sleeve has a curved armhole shaping on the body and a curved upper portion—the cap—on the sleeve itself. Because the angles of these curves do not match exactly, you have to do some manipulation to smoothly set the sleeve in the armhole. Typically, the sleeve cap is 1½ to 2" (3.8–5 cm) shorter than the armhole depth, and the curve is more dramatic than the armhole curve.

To set in a sleeve, work with right sides together, match the sleeve seam to the side seam, and pin in place. Mark the center top of the sleeve cap and match to the shoulder seam. Pin in place. Gradually pin the areas inbetween, easing the fit as necessary. Sew in place with a backstitch, which allows more control and flexibility than crocheted stitches.

POCKET

With hook and yarn, loosely ch 27 sts. *Sc 26 sts, turn. Ch 1*. Rep from * to * for 2 more rows (3 sc rows). Starting with Row 1 of main patt (wrong side) work in patt st over 26 sts until pocket measures 4½" (11.5 cm) from beg ch. Work 3 rows in sc. Fasten off.

FINISHING

Block pieces to size. With right sides together and size E/4 (3.5 mm) hook, slip-stitch crochet shoulders and sides of neck together. Measure down 9 (9½, 9½, 10¼)" (23 [24, 24, 26] cm) from shoulder seam and mark with safety pin or contrast yarn to indicate armhole depth. Mark center top of each sleeve with pin or contrast yarn. With right sides together pin sleeve to body of sweater matching center top of sleeve to shoulder seam and edges of sleeve top to markers along sides of sweater. With sleeve side of work facing and using sc sts as spacing guide, work slip-stitch crochet seam along the armhole attaching sleeve to body. With threaded tapestry needle backstitch side and sleeve seams as one, leaving the seam open at the 3 sc rows at the bottom edge of both body and sleeves. Pin pocket on front left side, with the top edge of the pocket positioned 7" (18 cm) down from shoulder and the pocket right-side edge 3" (7.5 cm) from center front. With threaded tapestry needle, whipstitch pocket in place, working along both sides and across the lower pocket edge. Take care not to catch the back when attaching pocket to front. Remove pins. Weave in any loose yarn tails to wrong side of work.

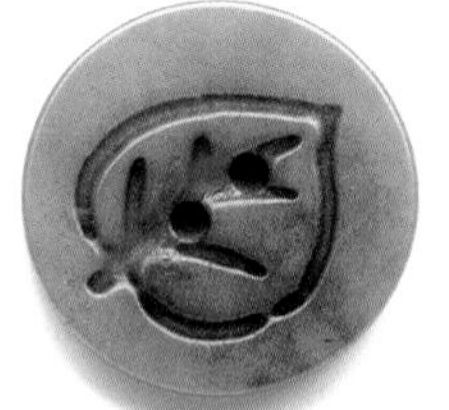

ON-THE-SIDE

CARDIGAN

Not only is this sweater incredibly cozy, its simple lacy stitch and band of repeated motifs make it one magnificent, all-out feminine cardigan. The asymmetrical closing adds even more flair.

S P E C I F I C A T I O N S

SIZE

To fit 34 (38, 42, 46)" (86.5 [96.5, 106.5, 117] cm) bust circumference. Actual measurements 40 (44, 48, 52)" (101.5 [112, 122, 132] cm) bust circumference; 22 (25, 26, 28)" (56 [63.5, 66, 71] cm) length. Sweater shown measures 44" (112 cm).

YARN

About 1400 (1600, 1800, 2000) yd (1280 [1463, 1646, 1829] m) double-knitting weight yarn. ***We used:*** Classic Elite Miracle (50% alpaca, 50% tencel; 108 yd [98m]/50 g): 13 (15, 17, 19) skeins #3306 taupe.

HOOK

Size E/4 (3.5mm) and size G/6 (4mm). Adjust hook size if necessary to obtain the correct gauge.

NOTIONS

Three buttons about ¾" (2 cm) in diameter; tapestry needle; safety pins, T-pins, or long sewing pins.

GAUGE

21 stitches and 8.25 rows = 4" (10 cm) worked in Three plus Two Stitch pattern with size G/6 (4mm) hook; 1 motif = 3" (7.5 cm) square worked with size G/6 (4 mm) hook; 1 motif = 2½" (6.5 mm) square worked with size E/4 (3.5 mm) hook.

ABBREVIATIONS

beg—beginning
ch—chain
dc—double crochet
dc2tog—double crochet 2 together
dc3tog—double crochet 3 together
est—established
hdc—half double crochet
hk—hook
lp—loop
patt—pattern
RS—right side (of work)
rep—repeat
sk—skip
sl st—slip stitch
sp(s)—space(s)
st(s)—stitch(es)

Review Basics, page 2:
Chain stitch
Decreasing
Double crochet
Half double crochet
Increasing
Reading a pattern
Seaming
Weaving in ends

If only you could feel this yarn right now–yummy!

PATTERN STITCHES

Three plus Two Stitch: Worked over a multiple of 6 + 2 stitches (add 2 for base chain). Pattern is the same on both sides.

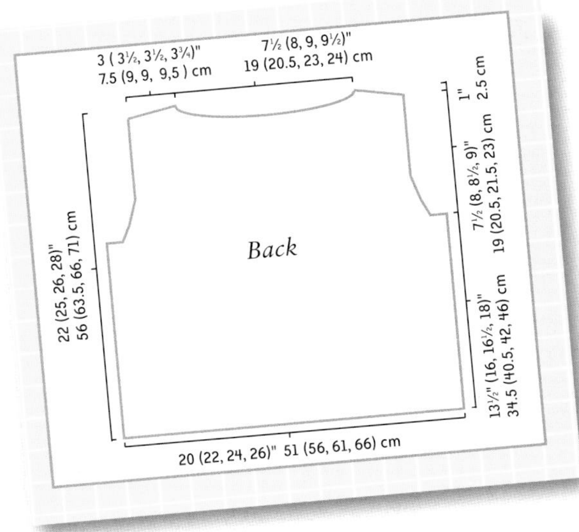

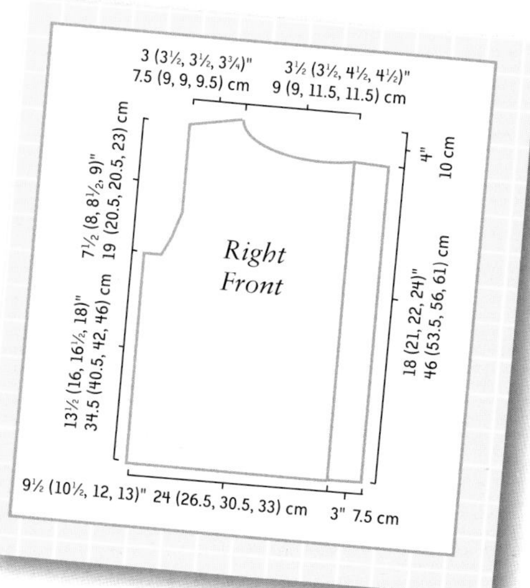

Row 1: Work a V-st [1 dc, 1 ch, 1 dc] into the fifth chain from hook, *sk 2 ch, 3 dc into next ch, sk 2 ch, work a V-st into next ch*; rep from * to * to last 5 chs, sk 2 chs, 3 dc into next ch, sk 1 ch, 1 dc into last ch, turn.

Row 2: Ch 3, *sk 2 sts, work 3 dc into center dc of next 3 dc sts, work a V-st into ch sp at center of next V-st*; rep from * to * ending 1 dc in top of turning ch, turn.

Row 3: Ch 3, *V-st into ch sp of next V-st, 3 dc into center dc of next 3 dc*; rep from * to * ending row with 1 dc in top of turning ch, turn.

Rep Rows 2 and 3 for patt.

Motif: With hook and yarn, ch 4 sts. Join into a ring as follows (see page 23): Insert hook into first ch and join with sl st to lp on hook.

Rnd 1: Ch 2, work 12 hdc in ring, join rnd with sl st to top of ch 2.

Rnd 2: Ch 3, work 1 dc2tog in same sp as ch 3 (counts as dc3tog), [ch 2, work 1 dc3tog in next st] 2 times, ch 3, *(work 1 dc3tog in next st, ch 2) 2 times, work 1 dc3tog, ch 3*; rep from * to * 2 more times, join rnd by working 1 dc into top of ch 3.

Rnd 3: Ch 3 (counts as 1 dc), work (2 dc, ch 3, 3 dc) in ch 3 sp, *work (1 dc, ch 1, 1 dc) in each of next 2 ch 2 sps*, work (3 dc, ch 3, 3 dc) into ch 3 sp**; rep from * to* * 2 more times, then rep from * to * one time, join with sl st to top of beg ch 3. Fasten off.

Make 6 (13, 13, 16) motifs using size G/6 (4 mm) hook (large motif) and 15 (10, 10, 10) motifs using size E/4 (3.5 mm) hook (small motif).

BACK

With size G/6 (4 mm) hook and yarn, loosely ch 106 (118, 130, 142) sts. Work Row 1 of Three plus Two Stitch pattern—104 (116, 128, 140) sts. Work Rows 2 and 3 of patt until back measures a total length of 13½ (16, 16½, 18)" (34.5 [40.5, 42, 46] cm). Do not work turning ch at beg of next row. ***Shape armhole:*** Sl st across first 5 (6, 6, 7) sts, ch 3, work in patt st as est to last 5 (6, 6, 7) sts, turn.

Next Row: Sl st across the first 4 (5, 5, 6)sts, ch 3, work in est patt to last 4 (5, 5, 6) sts, turn.

Next Row: Sl st across first 3 (3, 3, 3) sts, ch 3, work in patt to last 3 (3, 3, 3) sts, turn.

Next Row: Sl st across first 2 (2, 3, 3) sts, ch 3, work in patt to last 2 (2, 3, 3) sts, turn.

Next Row: Sl st across 1 (1, 2, 3) sts, ch 3, work in patt to last 1 (1, 2, 3) sts, turn.

Next Row: Sl st across 1 st, ch 3, work in patt across row until 1 st remains, turn. Rep last row 0 (1, 2, 2) more times—72 (78, 84, 90) sts.

Work even in patt on the remaining sts until armhole measures 7½ (8, 8½, 9)" (19 [20.5, 21.5, 23] cm). ***Shape neck and shoulders:*** On next row sl st across first 6 sts, ch 3, work in est patt over next 16 (18, 18, 20) sts, turn.

Next Row: Sl st across first 6 sts at neck edge, ch 3, work in patt to the last 5 (6, 6, 7) sts, turn.

Next Row: Ch 3, work 5 (6, 6, 7) sts. Fasten off as follows: Cut yarn leaving 4" (10 cm) tail, insert tail through last lp on hook and pull to tighten.
Reattach yarn 6 sts from opposite shoulder edge, ch 3. Work in est patt over next 16 (18, 18, 20) sts, turn.
Next Row: Sl st across first 6 sts at neck edge, ch 3, work in patt to last 5 (6, 6, 7) sts, turn. Ch 3, work 5 (6, 6, 7) sts. Fasten off.

RIGHT FRONT

With larger hook and yarn, loosely ch 52 (58, 64, 70) sts. Work Row 1 of Three plus Two Stitch pattern—50 (56, 62, 68) sts. Work Rows 2 and 3 of patt until front measures the same length as back to underarm. Do not work turning ch at beg of next row. ***Shape armhole:*** On next row sl st across first 5 (6, 6, 7) sts, ch 3, continue in patt as est to end of row, turn.
Next Row: Ch 3, work in est patt to last 4 (5, 5, 6)sts, turn.
Next Row: Sl st across first 3 (3, 3, 3) sts, ch 3, work in patt to end, turn.
Next Row: Ch 3, work in est patt to last 2 (2, 3, 3) sts, turn.
Next Row: Sl st across 1 (2, 2, 2) sts, ch 3, work in patt to end, turn.
Next Row: Ch 3, work in est patt to last 1 (1, 1, 2) sts, turn.
For 2 larger sizes only: Decrease 1 st at armhole edge 2 more times. ***All sizes:*** Work even in est patt on 34 (37, 42, 43) sts until front measures 18 (21, 22, 24)" (46 [53.5, 56, 61] cm), ending at armhole edge. ***Shape Neck:*** Ch 3, work across next row in patt to last 6 (7, 8, 8) sts (neck edge) turn, sl st across first 4 (5, 6, 5) sts, ch 3, work in est patt to end, turn.
Next Row: Ch 3, work in patt to last 4 (4, 4, 4) sts, turn.

PICOT EDGE

A picot is a small loop or twist evenly spaced between single crochet stitches to form a subtle decorative edge. It adds a nice finishing touch and is very typical of traditional crochet. Picot edges are easy, and you can make the effect subtle or dramatic by varying both the distance between picots and the size of the picot itself.

A picot edge is best worked as a final row after at least one row of single crochet—it smooths out an edge that may be curved or jagged from shaping. Allow for several single crochet stitches between picots, usually at least 3, and proceed as follows: Work 3 (or more) single crochet, *chain 3 (Figure 1), work single crochet in next stitch to close the picot (Figure 2), work 3 (or more) single crochet *; repeat from * to* along edge. For a more pronounced picot, work as above but after the chain 3, work 1 slip stitch in the first chain to close the picot before you continue single crochet (Figure 3). For an even more pronounced picot, work a longer picot chain. For a subtler effect, work more single crochet stitches between picots.

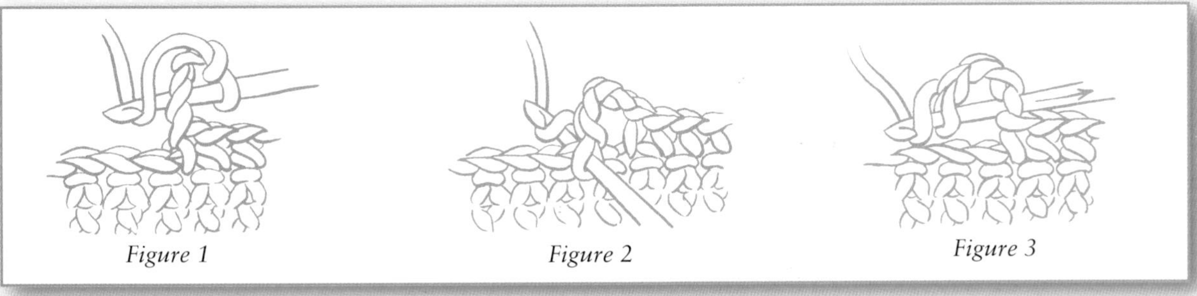
Figure 1 *Figure 2* *Figure 3*

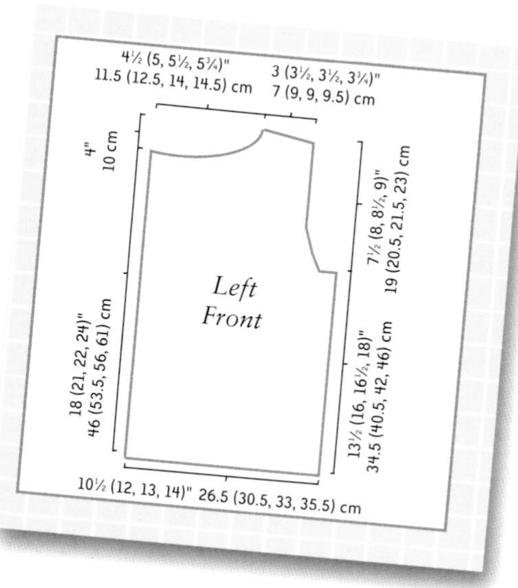

Next Row: Sl st across first 2 (1, 3, 3) sts, ch 3, work in patt to end, turn.
Next Row: Ch 3, work in patt to last 1 (1, 2, 2) sts, turn.
Next Row: Sl st across 1 st, ch 3, work in patt to end.
At the same time, when armhole measures 7½ (8, 8½, 9)" (19 [20.5, 21.5, 23] cm). ***Shape shoulder:*** At shoulder edge, sl st across first 6 sts, ch 3, work in patt to end. Ch 3, turn, work in patt to last 5 (6, 6, 7) sts, turn. Ch 3, work 5 (6, 6, 7) sts. Fasten off.

LEFT FRONT

With larger hook and yarn, loosely ch 58 (64, 70, 76) sts. Work Row 1 of Three plus Two Stitch pattern—56 (62, 68, 74) sts. Work Rows 2 and 3 of patt until front measures the same length as back to underarm. ***Shape armhole:*** Beg at the opposite edge, shape armhole same as the Right Front. Work even on 40 (43, 46, 51) sts until Front measures a total length of 18 (21, 22, 24)" (46 [53.5, 56, 61] cm). ***Shape neck:*** Beg at opposite edge from armhole, sl st across first 12 (14, 14, 15) sts, ch 3, work even in patt st as est to end of row, turn.
Next Row: Ch 3, work in patt to last 4 (4, 5, 5) sts, turn.
Next Row: Sl st across first 4 (4, 4, 4) sts, ch 3, work in est patt to end of row, turn.
Next Row: Ch 3, work in patt to last 2 (2, 3, 3) sts, turn.
Next Row: Sl st across 1 (1, 1, 1) st, ch 3, work in patt to end of row, turn.
Next Row: Ch 3, work in patt until last 1 (1, 1, 1) sts, turn.
Next Row: Ch 3, work in est patt to end of row—16 (18, 18, 20) sts.
At the same time, when front measures same as back to beg of shoulder shaping, shape shoulder same as Right Front.

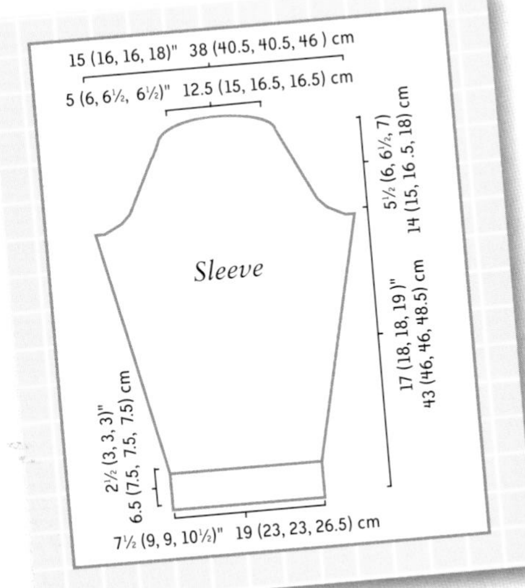

SLEEVES

(Make 2) With RS of work facing, whipstitch 3 small (3 large, 3 large, 4 large) motifs together. With larger hook and RS facing, work 44 (50, 50, 56) sc evenly across the top of the motifs' long edge. Then work 1 row as follows: Ch 3 (counts as 1 dc), work a V-st of [1 dc, 1 ch, 1 dc] into 3rd sc, *sk 2 sc, 3 dc into next sc, sk 2 sc, work a V-st into next sc*. Rep from * to * to last 5 sc, sk 2 sc, 3 dc into next sc, sk 1 sc, 1 dc into last sc, turn—44 (50, 50, 56) sts. Continue working Rows 2 and 3 according to patt st.

Note: For the following sleeve shaping, make increases by working an extra dc in the same st as the edge ch 3 or dc. Work these sts as dc sts until you have enough stitches to work a patt rep, then work the extra sts in patt. Beg with next row (Row 3), inc 1 st at each edge every row 8 (10, 10, 11) times, *then every other row* 8 times for a total of 76 (86, 86, 94) sts. Work even until sleeve measures 17 (18, 18, 19)" (43 [46, 46, 48.5] cm) in length, including motif.

Note: To prevent row gauge from stretching during the cap shaping, support the sleeve weight as you work.

Shape cap: Sl st across first 5 (6, 6, 7) sts of next row, ch 3, work in est patt to last 5 (6, 6, 7) sts, turn.
Next Row: Sl st across first 4 (5, 5, 6) sts, ch 3, work in est patt to last 4 (5, 5, 6) sts, turn.
Next Row: Sl st across first 3 (4, 3, 4) sts, ch 3, work in est patt as est to last 3 (4, 3, 4) sts, turn.

Next Row: Sl st across first 3 (3, 3, 3) sts, ch 3, work in est patt to last 3 (3, 3, 3) sts, turn.
Next Row: Sl st across 1 (3, 2, 3) sts, ch 3, work in est patt to last 1 (3, 2, 3) sts, turn.
Next Row: Sl st across 1 (2, 2, 2) sts, ch 3, work in est patt to last 1 (2, 2, 2) sts, turn.
Next Row: Sl st across 1 (1, 2, 2) sts, ch 3, work in est patt to last 1 (1, 2, 2) sts, turn.
Next Row: Sl st across first 2 (1, 1, 1) sts, ch 3, work in est patt to last 2 (1, 1, 1) sts, turn.
Next Row: Sl st across first 2 (1, 1, 1) sts, ch 3, work in est patt to last 2 (1, 1, 1) sts, turn.
Next Row: Sl st across first 3 (1, 1, 1) sts, ch 3, work in est patt to last 3 (1, 1, 1) sts, turn—26 (32, 34, 34) sts. Work even until cap measures about 5½ (6, 6½, 7)" (14 [15, 16.5, 18,] cm) from beg of armhole shaping. Fasten off.

FINISHING

Using larger hook and yarn, with RS of work together, sl st shoulder seams, side seams and sleeve seams. ***Attach sleeves to armhole:*** Pin sleeve cap into armhole (see page 74), matching seams at bottom and matching center top of sleeve to shoulder seam, easing to fit as necessary. With threaded tapestry needle, sew sleeve in place using backstitch. ***Center Front Panel:*** With RS facing, using whipstitch, sew 6 (7, 7, 8) large motifs into a strip. Sew strip to center front of right front. ***Neckline border:*** With smaller hook, work 1 row sc evenly around neck edge, smoothing out jogs from shaping. With RS of work facing, whipstitch together 9 (10, 10, 10) small motifs. Pin motifs to neck edge, aligning first motif with top vertical motif on right front, then pin motifs at shoulder seams, and center back, ease neck edge to fit as necessary. Whipstitch motifs to neck. Remove pins. Using safety pins, mark placement of three buttonholes placing top buttonhole at top edge of collar, second buttonhole at bottom of collar motif and third buttonhole at bottom of second motif. Beg at either side seam at lower edge, with smaller hook attach yarn, ch 1, work 1 row sc evenly around lower edge, center fronts and neck edge, working 1 st each in st or chains along horizontal edges and spacing sts evenly on vertical edges to prevent edge from rippling. Join with sl st to beg ch. Work picot rnd (see page 79) as follows: Ch 1, work 1 sc in each of first 3 sc, *ch 3, work 1 sc in each of next 3 sc*; rep from * to * around, working buttonholes as marked on right front. To work buttonholes (see page 71), ch 3, skip 3 sts and resume patt as est in fourth st. **Note:** Work picots before and after buttonholes, even though there will be an extra stitch between them. Join to top of beg ch with sl st. Fasten off. With smaller hook attach yarn at sleeve seam, ch 1, work 42 (45, 45, 54) sc around lower edge of sleeve (motifs), join to beg ch with sl st. Work *picot rnd* as follows: Ch 1, work 1 sc in each of first 3 sc, *ch 3, work 1 sc in each of next 3 sc*; rep from * to * around, join with sl st. Fasten off. With tapestry needle, weave in loose ends. Steam seams and block lightly as needed. Sew buttons (see page 74) opposite buttonholes.

BLOCK-ON-BLOCK

SKIRT

When has the granny square, the most familiar motif associated with modern crochet, been so hip? This lightweight skirt hangs just right. The drawstring allows for an easy fit at or below the waist. The yarn varies subtly in color, so no two squares are the same despite the fact that only four colors are used throughout.

SPECIFICATIONS

■ **SIZE**

S (M, L, XL); 36 (38, 40, 42)" (91.5 [96.5, 101.5, 106.5] cm) hip circumference; 38 (40, 42, 44)" (96.5 [101.5, 106.5] cm) hip circumference after blocking; 25 (26, 26, 27)" (63.5 [66, 66, 68.5] cm) length after blocking. Sample shown is size 40 (101.5 cm).

■ **YARN**

About 1500 (1600, 1700, 1850) yd [1385 (1475, 1570, 1710) m] sock-weight yarn. ***We used:*** Schoeller/Stahl Fortissima Colori Socka Color (75% superwash wool, 25% polyamid; 229 yd [210 m]/50 g); 3 skeins #2420 reds (A), 2 skeins each: #2418 greens (B), #2419 yellows/multi (C), #2417 blues (D). **Note:** The multiple colors mean that the number of skeins needed are the same for all sizes even though yardage amounts vary.

■ **HOOK**

Size B/1 (2.25mm), C/2 (2.75mm), D/3 (3.25mm). Adjust hook size if necessary to obtain the correct gauge.

■ **NOTIONS**

Tapestry needle; safety pins.

■ **GAUGE**

Small motif = 2¾" (7 cm) square with size B/1 (2.25 mm) hook; Medium motif = 2⅞" (7.25 cm) square with size C/2 (2.75 mm) hook; Large motif = 3" (7.5 cm) square with size D/3 (3.25 mm) hook. 22 stitches and 15 rows = 4" (10 cm) in double crochet with size B/1 (2.25 mm) hook.

■ **ABBREVIATIONS**

beg—begin, beginning
ch—chain
dc—double crochet
rep—repeat
sc—single crochet
sl st—slip stitch
sp—space(s)
st(s)—stitch(es)
yo—yarn over

Review Basics, page 2:
Chain stitch
Circular crochet
Decreasing
Double crochet
Reading a pattern
Weaving in ends

Chart for motif placement

3	4	1	2	3	4	1	2	3	4	1	2	3	4	1	2	Use crochet hook B/1 (2.25 mm) to make these motifs
2	3	4	1	2	3	4	1	2	3	4	1	2	3	4	1	
1	2	3	4	1	2	3	4	1	2	3	4	1	2	3	4	Use crochet hook C/2 (2.75 mm) to make these motifs
4	1	2	3	4	1	2	3	4	1	2	3	4	1	2	3	
3	4	1	2	3	4	1	2	3	4	1	2	3	4	1	2	
2	3	4	1	2	3	4	1	2	3	4	1	2	3	4	1	Use crochet hook D/3 (3.25 mm) to make these motifs
1	2	3	4	1	2	3	4	1	2	3	4	1	2	3	4	
XL	L	M	S												begin	

Color sequence for motifs

Motif 1: beg at center
(C) yellow
(A) red
(D) blue
(B) green

Motif 2: beg at center
(B) green
(C) yellow
(A) red
(D) blue

Motif 3: beg at center
(A) red
(D) blue
(B) green
(C) yellow

Motif 4: beg at center
(D) blue
(B) green
(C) yellow
(A) red

■ **GRANNY SQUARE MOTIF**

The motif is worked in four rounds that change color with each round. See charts for hook size per square, color placement within each square, and placement of finished squares. With first color, ch 4 sts, join with sl st to form ring (see page 23).

Rnd 1: Ch 3 (counts as 1 dc), work 2 dc in ring, *ch 2, work 3 dc in ring*; rep from * to * 2 more times, ch 2, join with sl st to top of ch 3. Fasten off as follows: Cut yarn leaving 4" (10 cm) tail, insert tail through last st on hook and pull to tighten and secure.

Rnd 2: Join second color to any ch-2 sp. Ch 3 (counts as 1 dc), into same sp work [2 dc, ch 2, 3 dc], *ch 1, into next ch-2 sp work [3 dc, ch 2, 3 dc]*; rep from * to * 2 more times, ch 1, join with sl st to top of ch 3. Fasten off.

Rnd 3: Join third color to any ch-2 sp. Ch 3 (counts as 1 dc), into same sp work [2 dc, ch

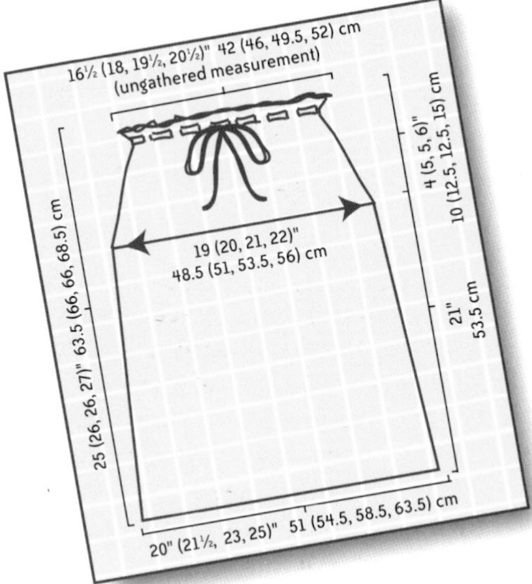

2, 3 dc], *ch 1, work 3 dc into next ch-1 sp, ch 1, work [3 dc, ch 2, 3 dc] into next ch-2 sp*; rep from * to * 2 more times, ch 1, work 3 dc in next ch-1 sp, ch 1, join with sl st to top of ch 3. Fasten off.

Rnd 4: Join fourth color to any ch-2 sp. Ch 3 (counts as 1 dc), into same sp work [2 dc, ch 2, 3 dc], *ch 1, work 3 dc into next ch-1 sp, ch 1, work 3 dc into next ch-1 sp, ch 1, work [3 dc, ch 2, 3 dc] into next ch-2 sp*; rep from * to * 2 more times, work 3 dc into next ch-1 sp, work 3 dc into next ch-1 sp, ch 1, join with sl st to top of ch 3. Fasten off.

Following the color chart, work as follows: With B/1 (2.25 m) hook make 26 (28, 30, 32) motifs With C/2 (2.75 mm) hook make 39 (42, 45, 48) motifs. With D/3 (3.25 mm) hook, make 26 (28, 30, 32) motifs.

Note: For ease in working, sew all the same hook-size squares together before starting the next hook-size squares. When all three groups of squares are attached to each other, assemble the three sections into one and then finish.

Assembling the motifs: Group the squares together by size. Working from the lower edge (hemline) upward, use the largest squares in the two lowest "rows," next the three "rows" of middle-size squares, followed by two "rows" of the smallest squares. The sc stitches for the hip yoke are worked into the smaller squares. With color A and tapestry needle, sew squares together. With right sides facing, butt the edges together and sew back and forth along each edge, matching the motifs stitch for stitch. Ease the edges together when you're sewing squares made with different hook sizes. When all the squares are attached, forming one large piece of fabric, sew the two side edges together to form a tube, using safety pins to hold edges in place. The seam is the center back. *Optional:* If you want more leg space at the lower edge, allow several inches of back seam to remain open and slip st along the motif side edges not included in the back seam. The lower edge border (see below) is then worked flat, back and forth, and not joined into a round.

FINISHING

Lower Edge: Beg at the center back, with size D/3 (3.25 mm) hook and color A, ch 1, sc 17 sts across each motif, working 1 row sc evenly around lower edge for a total of 221 (238, 255, 272) sts. Join sts into circle with a sl st. Ch 3, work 1 dc in each sc, join with sl st to top of ch 3. Fasten off. Attach color C at center back. Ch 3, work 1 dc between each dc of previous round, join with sl st to top of ch 3. Fasten off. Attach color D at center back and work the same as previous round, join with sl st to top of ch 3. Fasten off. Work should measure about 21" (53.5 cm) in length at this point.

Hip Yoke: Beg at the top of center back, with size B/1 (2.25 mm) hook and color A, join yarn, ch 1, work 1 row sc evenly around upper edge as follows:

Sizes S and M: Work 16 sc per square; *Size L:* Work 15 sc across 8 squares and 16 sc across 7 squares, alternating the number of sc worked (15 sc, 16 sc, 15 sc, 16 sc, 15 sc and so forth); *Size XL:* Work 15 sc per square.

Total number of sc sts—208 (224, 232, 240), join with sl st to ch 1.

Note: The decreases in the following dc section are worked as follows: Yo, insert hook into next st and pull up a loop (3 loops on hook), yo and pull through first 2 loops on the hook (2 loops remain on hook), yo, insert hook in next st, yo and pull up a loop (4 loops on hook), yo, and draw through first 2 loops on hook, (3 loops remain), yo, draw through all 3 loops on hook—1 loop remains on hook (1 dc decrease made).

Rnd 1: Ch 3 (counts as 1 dc), work 1 dc in each sc, join with sl st to top of ch 3.
Rnd 2: Ch 3 (counts as 1 dc), work 1 dc between each dc of the previous rnd, join with sl st to top of ch 3.
Rnd 3: (decrease rnd) Ch 3 (counts as 1 dc),work 1 dc between each dc same as for previous rnd, dec 9 (10, 6, 3) sts evenly spaced throughout the rnd, join with sl st to top of ch 3—199 (214, 226, 237) sts.
Rnds 4–5: Work same as Rnd 2.
Rnd 6: (decrease rnd) Ch 3 (counts as 1 dc), work 1 dc between each dc the same as previous rnd, dec 9 (8, 6, 3) sts evenly spaced throughout the rnd—190 (206, 220, 234) sts.
Rnds 7–9: Work same as Rnd 2.
Rnd 10: Ch 3 (counts as 1 dc), work 1 dc between each dc the same as previous rnd, dec 10 (11, 5, 4) sts evenly spaced throughout the rnd—180 (195, 215, 230) sts.
Next Rnd: Work same as Rnd 2—1 (5, 5, 9) times.
Eyelet rnd: Ch 3 (counts as 1 dc), work 1 dc in sp between next 2 sts, *ch 2, skip next 2 sps, work 1 dc between each of next 3 dc; rep from * to *, end rnd with 1 dc, join with sl st to top of ch 3.
Next rnd: Ch 3 (counts as 1 dc), work 1 dc between each dc as on previous rounds, and work 3 dc in ch-2 sps—180 (195, 215, 230). Fasten off.
Next rnd: At center back, attach color C. Ch 3 (counts as 1 dc), work 1 dc between each dc, join with sl st to top of ch 3. Fasten off.
Next rnd: At center back attach color D and work same as previous round. Fasten off. Work should measure about 4 (5, 5, 6)" (10 [12.5, 12.5, 15] cm) in length from start of hip yoke, and total skirt length about 25 (26, 26, 27)" (63.5 [66, 66, 68.5] cm).
Weave in all loose ends to wrong side of work and secure.

■ DRAWSTRING

With size D/3 (3.25 mm) hook and 2 strands of color A, ch 300 (325, 350, 400) sts. Turn, work 1 sl st in each ch (see page 5). Fasten off. Attach safety pin to one end of drawstring and thread drawstring through eyelets. Adjust to fit waist or below waist as desired.
Tassel Ends: With size D/3 (3.25 mm) hook attach color C to one end of drawstring. Ch 3, work 2 dc in same sp, *ch 2, work 3 dc in same sp*; rep from * to * one more time, ch 2, join with sl st to top of ch 3. Fasten off. Rep at opposite end of drawstring. Weave in loose ends to wrong side of work and secure. Block skirt to measurements shown, or desired size.

GRADUATING HOOK SIZE

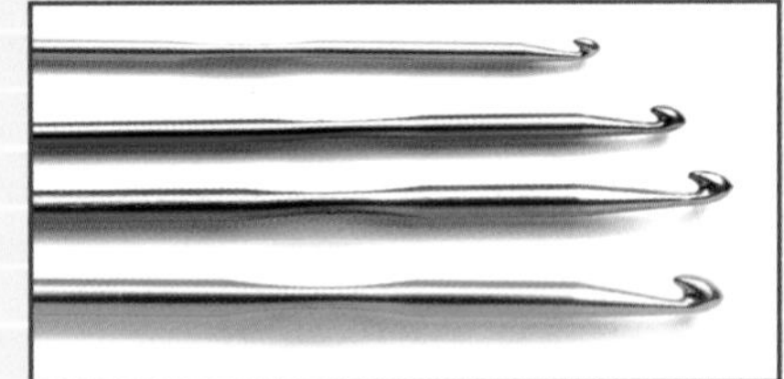

Varying hook size is an easy way to add subtle shaping to any crocheted item. Each item usually has an optimum hook size, determined by its yarn, gauge, and intended use. It stands to reason that, with the same yarn, a small hook creates a stiff fabric while a large hook creates a loose fabric. For example, a scarf will often require a larger hook than a sweater made from the same yarn because a scarf needs more drape than a sweater. Crochet stitches can also dictate hook size. In general, a simple single-crochet fabric requires a larger hook than a stitch pattern composed of double crochet or long stitches. Keeping all this in mind, it is possible to work with a hook one or two sizes larger or smaller than the optimum without compromising the integrity of the fabric. In this way you can add subtle shaping to a piece where normal increasing or decreasing would interfere with the line of the pattern.

In a skirt, such as the Block-on-Block Skirt, using a large hook at the bottom and gradually changing to smaller hooks adds a slight A-line shape without disturbing the line of the design—the number of motifs can stay constant while the skirt develops a flattering shape. In a body-skimming fitted sweater, start with a large hook at the hipline, work down to a smaller hook at the waist, and then work back to a large hook at the bust. On a collar you can use a small hook close to the neck, then gradually change to larger hooks so a cowl or spread collar lies flat.

Changing hook size throughout a garment can increase or decrease the garment one whole size. Follow the rule—make swatches, measure carefully, and calculate the finished size before you start.

GIRLY-GIRL

CAPELET

As feminine as can be, as light as a whisper, this capelet has vintage and contemporary appeal at the same time. The stitches are deceptively simple to learn, yet in combination their lacy effect is intriguingly complex.

SIZE

16" (40.5 cm) length; 54" (137 cm) circumference at lower edge; 22" (56 cm) circumference at neck edge.

YARN

Fine-weight mohair, about 1250 yd (1155 m). *We used:* Rowan's Kidsilk Haze (70% superkid mohair, 30% silk; 229 yd [210m]/25 g): 6 balls #600 dewberry.

HOOK

Crochet hooks size C/2 (2.75 mm), D/3 (3.25 mm), E/4 (3.5 mm). Adjust hook size if necessary to obtain the correct gauge.

NOTIONS

Three buttons, about ½" (1.3 cm) in diameter; tapestry needle.

GAUGE

19 stitches and 12 rounds = 4" (10 cm) worked in double crochet with two strands held together with size E/4 (3.5 mm) hook.

ABBREVIATIONS

beg—beginning
ch—chain
dc—double crochet
rep—repeat
sc—single crochet
sk—skip
sl st—slip stitch (crochet)
sp—space(s)
st(s)—stitch(es)

Review Basics, page 2:
Chain stitch
Double crochet
Reading a pattern
Single crochet
Slip stitch
Weaving in ends
Working in rounds

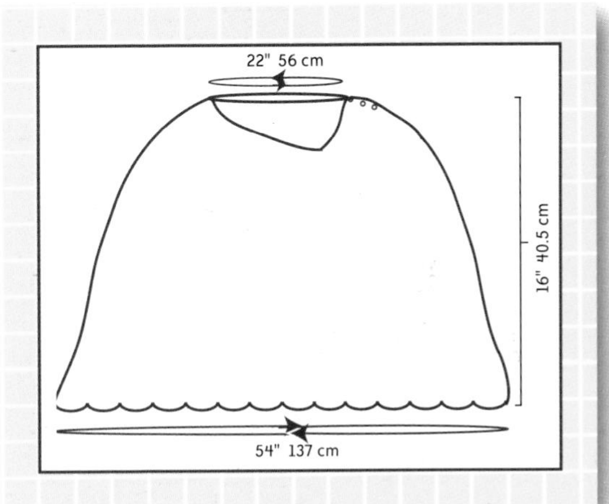

STITCHES

Trellis Stitch Insert: (Rounds Version, worked in three-round insert over 256 sts)

Multiple of 4 sts

Rnd 1: *Ch 5, sk 3 sts, 1 sc in next st*; rep from * to * to end of rnd, work 1 sc in same st as starting ch.

Rnd 2: Ch 3, *work 1 sc in ch-5 sp, ch 5*; rep from * to * around, end with ch 3, join with sl st (see page 6) to beg ch 3.

Rnd 3: 1 sc in same sp as last ch, *ch 3, work 1 sc in ch-5 sp*; rep from * to * around, join to beg.

Trellis Stitch: (Rows Version, worked over 106 sts)

Multiple of 4 sts + 3 (add 3 for base chain)

Row 1: 1 sc into sixth ch from hook, *ch 5, sk 3 ch, 1 sc in next ch*; rep from * to * across. Turn.

Row 2: *Ch 5, 1 sc into next 5-ch sp*; rep from * to * across.

Rep Row 2 for pattern.

LACE CROCHET

Crochet is the ideal technique for creating lace. While solid fabrics in crochet can become stiff and heavy, the openness of lace adds lightness and drape. Fine yarns make especially beautiful lace. The techniques for making lace stitches vary, but it is often common to work stitches into spaces rather than into other stitches. It's not easy working into tiny stitches, so working into spaces is a big plus when you're using a fine yarn and small hook.

In traditional crochet, finely worked lace tablecloths and bedspreads become heirloom pieces. While these larger pieces are usually created in motifs for ease in working, smaller pieces are often created as a single piece. Edgings are another traditional application for crocheted lace. Narrow bands of lace add a charming touch to linen towels and pillowcases.

Filet Crochet and Irish Crochet are two popular forms of crocheted lace. Filet crochet is a simple combination of double crochet and chain stitches. The placement of these stitches creates intricate patterns, from simple shapes to words to complete scenes. In Irish Crochet, separate elaborate motifs are combined with an openwork crocheted net or mesh ground fabric to create a unique and distinctive effect.

In a luxurious yarn, even the simplest combination of stitches and chains can create a beautiful lace fabric. Start out simply. Once you understand the concept of creating lace, the possibilities become limitless.

Shell Network: (Rounds Version, worked over 256 sts)
Multiple of 8 sts
Rnd 1: Ch 4 (counts as 1 dc and 1 ch), sk first st and next ch, 1 dc into next dc, *sk 2 dc, 5 dc into next dc, skip 2 dc, 1 dc into next dc, ch 1, 1 dc into next dc*; rep from * to * around, join to third ch of beg ch 4.
Rep Rnd 1 for pattern.
Border Pattern: (Rounds Version, worked over 256 sts)
Multiple of 8 sts
Rnd 1: Ch 3 (counts as 1 dc), work 1 dc in each st, join with sl st to top of ch 3 (see Page 6).
Rnd 2: Ch 1, work 1 sc in each of first 3 dc, *sk next dc, ch 2, work (2 dc, ch 2, 2 dc) in next dc, ch 2, sk next dc, work 1 sc in each of next 5 dc*; rep from * to * around, end sc 2, join with sl st to ch.
Rnd 3: Ch 1, work 1 sc in each of next 2 sc, *ch 3, sk first ch-2 sp, in second ch-2 sp work (3 dc, ch 2, 3 dc), ch 3, sk next ch-2 sp and 1 sc, work 1 sc in each of next 3 sc*; rep from * to * around, end 1 sc, join with sl st to ch.
Rnd 4: Ch 1, work 1 sc in first sc, *ch 4, sk next ch-3 sp, in ch-2 sp work (4 dc, ch 2, 4 dc), ch 4, sk 1 sc, work 1 sc in next sc*; rep from * to * around, join to ch.
Fasten off.

CAPELET

Beg at the neck edge, with size E/4 (3.5 mm) hook and 2 strands of yarn held together, ch 106 sts.
Row 1: Beg in the second ch from hook and work 1 sc in each ch—105 sts. Turn.
Row 2: Ch 3 (counts as 1 dc), sk first sc, work 1 dc in each sc across row. Turn.
Row 3: Ch 3 (counts as 1 dc), sk first dc, work 1 dc in each of next 2 dc, work 2 dc in next dc, *work 1 dc in each of next 8 dc, work 2 dc in next dc*; rep from * to * across row to last 2 sts, end row working 1 dc in each of last 2 sts—117 sts. Turn.
Row 4: Ch 3 (counts as 1 dc), sk first dc, work 1 dc in each of next 2 dc, work 2 dc in next dc, *work 1 dc in each of next 9 dc, work 2 dc in next dc*; rep from * to * across row to last 3 sts, end row working 1 dc in each of last 3 sts—129 sts. Turn.
Row 5: Ch 3 (counts as 1 dc), sk first dc, work 1 dc in each of next 3 dc, work 2 dc in next dc, *work 1 dc in each of next 10 dc, work 2 dc in next dc*; rep from * to * across row to last 3 sts, end row working 1 dc in each of last 3 sts—141 sts. Turn.
Row 6: Ch 3 (counts as 1 dc), sk first dc, work 1 dc in each of next 3 dc, work 2 dc in next dc, *work 1 dc in each of next 11 dc, work 2 dc in next dc*; rep from * to * across row to last 4 sts, end row working 1 dc in each of last 4 sts—153 sts. Turn.
Row 7: Ch 3 (counts as 1 dc), sk first dc, work 1 dc in each of next 3 dc, work 2 dc in next dc, *work 1 dc in each of next 12 dc, work 2 dc in next dc*; rep from * to * across row to last 5 sts, end row working 1 dc in each of last 5 sts—165 sts. Do not turn.
Join with sl st to opposite end and begin working in rounds.
Rnd 1: Ch 3 (counts as 1 dc), sk first dc, work 1 dc in each of next 4 dc, work 2 dc in next dc*; work 1 dc in each of next 13 dc, work 2 dc in next dc*; rep from * to * to last 5 sts, end rnd with 1 dc in each of last 5 sts, join with sl st to top of ch 3—177 sts.
Rnd 2: Ch 3 (counts as 1 dc), sk first dc, work 1 dc in each of next 5 dc, work 2 dc

in next dc, *work 1 dc in each of next 14 dc, work 2 dc in next dc*; rep from * to * to last 5 sts, end rnd with 1 dc in each of last 5 sts, join with sl st to top of ch 3—189 sts.
Rnd 3: Ch 3 (counts as 1 dc), sk first dc, work 1 dc in each of next 6 dc, work 2 dc in next dc, *work 1 dc in each of next 15 dc, work 2 dc in next dc*; rep from * to * to last 5 sts, end rnd with 1 dc in each of last 5 sts, join with sl st to top of ch 3 sts—201 sts.
Rnd 4: Ch 3 (counts as 1 dc), sk first dc, work 1 dc in each of next 7 dc, work 2 dc in next dc, *work 1 dc in each of next 16 dc, work 2 dc in next dc*; rep from * to * to last 5 sts, end rnd with 1 dc in each of last 5 sts, join with sl st to top of ch 3—213 sts.
Rnd 5: Ch 3 (counts as 1 dc), sk first dc, work 1 dc in each of next 8 dc, work 2 dc in next dc, *work 1 dc in each of next 17 dc, work 2 dc in next dc*; rep from * to * to last 5 sts, end rnd with 1 dc in each of last 5 sts, join with sl st to top of ch 3—225 sts.
Rnd 6: Ch 3 (counts as 1 dc), sk first dc, work 1 dc in each of next 9 dc, work 2 dc in next dc, *work 1 dc in each of next 18 dc, work 2 dc in next dc*; rep from * to * to last 5 sts, end rnd with 1 dc in each of the last 5 dc, join with sl st to top of ch 3—237 sts.
Rnd 7: Ch 3 (counts as 1 dc), sk first dc, work 1 dc in each of next 10 dc, work 2 dc in next dc, *work 1 dc in each of next 19 dc, work 2 dc in next dc*; rep from * to * to last 5 sts, end rnd with 1 dc in each of the last 5 dc, join with sl st to top of ch 3—249 sts.
Rnd 8: Ch 3 (counts as 1 dc), sk first dc, work 1 dc in each of next 34 dc, work 2 dc in next dc, *work 1 dc in each of next 35 dc, work 2 dc in next st, work 1 dc in next 34 dc, work 2 dc in next st*; rep from * to * 2 more times, join with sl st to top of ch 3—256 sts.
Rnds 9–11: Work Trellis Stitch Insert (Rounds Version) over 256 sts.
Rnd 12: Ch 3 (counts as 1 dc), work 3 dc in each ch-3 sp, and 1 dc in each sc, join with sl st to top of ch.
Rnds 13–19: Work Shell Network stitch.
Rnd 20: Ch 3 (counts as 1 dc), work rnd in dc, working 1 dc into each dc sts and ch, join with sk st to top of ch.
Rnds 21–23: Work Trellis Stitch Insert (Rounds Version).
Rnd 24: Ch 3 (counts as 1 dc), work 3 dc in each ch-3 sp and 1 dc in each sc.
Border Pattern: Work 4 rnds in Border Pattern. Fasten off as follows: Cut yarn leaving 4" (10 cm) tail, insert tail through last lp on hook and pull to tighten.

Here are some other fun trellis stitches

Circle trellis stitch

Fan trellis stitch

Shell trellis stitch

FINISHING

Placket: With size C/2 (2.75 mm) hook, attach yarn at back neck edge, work 15 sc evenly down the back edge of the opening, 1 sc in corner and 15 sc along edge of front opening. Turn. Ch 1, *for buttonholes*, (see page 71) work 1 sc in first sc, *ch 3, sk 2 sc, work 1 sc in each of next 3 sc*; rep from * to * 2 more times, work the remaining sts in sc. Fasten off.
Collar: With size C/2 (2.75 mm) hook, attach yarn at front neck edge. Work 3 rows in Trellis Stitch (Rows Version) over the 106 neck edge sts. Change to size D/3 (3.25 mm) hook and continuing in Trellis Stitch work 3 more rows. Change to size E/4 (3.5 mm) hook and work 3 more rows in Trellis Stitch.
Edging: On next row work 5 sc into each ch-5 sp and 1 sc in each sc for edging. Fasten off.
Sew buttons opposite buttonholes. Steam or lightly block to size.

BOHEMIAN COAT

SWEATER

This coat pays homage to the exuberant crochet of the 1970s. Although the motif on the back is derived from a vest pattern of the times, it's been reinterpreted into a contemporary style that's fun and timeless. The Afghan-stitch cuffs and front band are embroidered with flowers that echo the back motif. Stripes carry the colors throughout the garment. For the classicist, instructions are also included for a plain back.

■ **SIZE**

S (M, L, XL) to fit 34 (38, 42, 46)" (86.5 [96.5, 106.5, 117] cm) bust circumference. Actual measurements 40 (44, 48, 52)" (101.5 [112, 122, 132] cm) bust circumference; 29 (30, 30, 31)" (73.5 [76, 76, 79] cm) length. Sweater shown measures 38" (96.5 cm).

■ **YARN**

Worsted-weight yarn, about 2400 (2500, 2600, 2800) yd (2195 [2286, 2378, 2561] m). ***We used:*** Classic Elite Wings (55% alpaca, 23% silk, 22% wool; 109 yards [100 m]/50 g): 11 (12, 13, 15) skeins #2377 charcoal (MC); 2 skeins each #2346 aqua (A), #2395 purple (B), #2307 thistle (C), #2327 plum (D); 1 skein each #2358 red (E), #2303 dove (F), #2310 navy (G).

■ **HOOK**

Size H/8 (5 mm) crochet hook; size H/8 (5 mm) afghan hook. Adjust hook size if necessary to obtain the correct gauge.

■ **NOTIONS**

Tapestry needle for embroidery, sewing together; safety pins or T-pins for holding pieces together.

■ **GAUGE**

15 stitches and 7 rows = 4" (10 cm) in double crochet with size H/8 (5 mm) hook. 16 stitches and 16 rows = 4" (10 cm) in basic Afghan stitch with size H/8 (5 mm) afghan hook. Finished back motif = 13" (33 cm) square.

■ **ABBREVIATIONS**

beg—begins, beginning
ch—chain
dc—double crochet
ddc—double double crochet
inc—increase
MC—main color
RS—right side of work
sc—single crochet
sk—skip
sl st—slip stitch
sp—space
st(s)—stitch(es)
tr—treble crochet
WS—wrong side of work

Review Basics, page 2:
Chain Stitch
Double crochet
Increases
Reading a pattern
Single crochet
Slip stitch
Treble crochet
Weaving in ends

■ **SPECIAL STITCHES**

Hold back the last loop of dc: Holding back the last loop of 2 or more dc stitches to combine them into a cluster. Work as follows: *Yarn over, insert hook into next stitch or space, yarn over and draw up a loop, yarn over and draw through 2 loops (2 loops remain on hook); rep from *. Rep this process the desired number of times

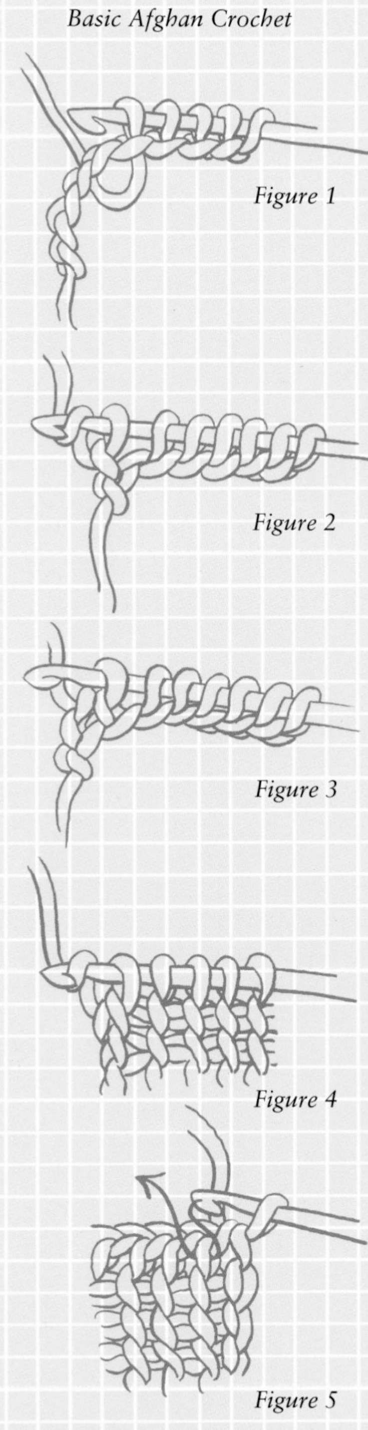

Figure 1
Figure 2
Figure 3
Figure 4
Figure 5

adding an extra loop for each partially worked dc, then wrap the yarn around the hook and pull through all the loops on the hook to close.

Double Double Crochet (ddc): Yarn over hook 3 times, insert the hook into st or sp, yarn over hook and pull through (5 loops on hook), *yarn over hook and pull through 2 loops*; work from * to * 4 times.

PATTERN STITCHES

Basic Afghan Crochet: *Foundation:* Using the afghan hook, chain desired length.
Base Row (part 1): Count the lp on the hook as the first st. Skip the ch nearest the hook, *Insert the hook in the next ch, wrap the yarn around the hook (yarn over) and draw up a loop; rep from * in each chain—the resulting stitches remain on the hook (Figure 1). Do not turn the work at the end of row.
Base Row (part 2): This row is worked in reverse, from left to right, and completes the first row. Yarn over and draw through the first loop (Figure 2). *Yarn over and draw through next 2 loops*; rep from * to * across row to last loop (Figure 3). One loop remains, which counts as the first stitch of the next row.
Row 1 (part 1): *Working from right to left insert the hook under the vertical bars formed by the previous second base row, yarn over and draw up loop; rep from * across row (Figure 4).
Row 1 (part 2): Working from left to right, yarn over, draw through first loop. *Yarn over hook, draw through next 2 loops; rep from * across row (Figure 5).
Rep both parts of Row 1 to desired length. Fasten off.
Edging Stitch: Attach yarn at corner of work. Work 1 sc in same sp. *Ch 4, skip next st, work 1 sc in next st*; rep from * to * along the edge. Fasten off.

Motif: With hook and color E, ch 3 sts. Join into a ring as follows (see page 6): Insert hook into first ch and join with sl st to lp on hook.
Rnd 1: Ch 3, work 15 dc in ring, join with sl st to top of ch 3.
Rnd 2: Ch 5, work 1 dc in same st (top of ch 3), *sk next st, work [1 dc, ch 2, 1 dc] in second dc*; rep from * to * 6 more times. Join with sl st to third ch of ch 5. Fasten off.
Rnd 3: Attach color D in any ch-2 sp. Ch 3, work 3 dc in same ch-2 sp, *ch 1, work 4 dc in next ch-2 sp*; rep from * to * 6 more times, end with ch 1. Join with sl st to top of ch 3.
Rnd 4: Ch 3, holding back the last loop of each dc, work 1 dc in each of next 3 dc (4 loops remain on hook), holding back the last loop, work 1 dc in ch-1 sp (5 loops remain on hook), yarn over hook and pull through all 5 loops, ch 4, work 1 dc in same ch-1 sp. *Holding back the last loop of each dc, work 1 dc in each of the next 4 dc (there are 5 loops on hook),

holding back the last loop, work 1 dc in ch-1 sp (there are now 6 loops on hook), yarn over hook and pull through all 6 loops, ch 4, work 1 dc in same ch-1 sp*; rep from * to * 6 more times. Join with sl st to the stitch above ch 3. Fasten off.

Petals: The petals are worked in rows, back and forth. One petal is worked in each ch-4 loop. Always start Row 1 with RS of work facing.
Row 1: Attach color C to any ch-4 sp. Ch 3, work 3 dc in same ch-4 sp, ch 2, work 4 dc in same ch-4 sp.
Row 2: Ch 1, turn, work 1 sc in second dc, ch 3, work 1 dc in each of next 2 dc, work [4 dc, ch 2, 4 dc] in ch-2 sp. Holding back the last loop of each dc, work 1 dc in each of next 3 dc (4 loops remain on hook), yarn over hook and pull through all 4 loops.
Row 3: Ch 1, turn, work 1 sc in fourth dc, ch 3, holding back the last loops of each dc work 1 dc in each of next 2 dc (3 loops remain on hook), yarn over hook and pull through all 3 loops, (sk last dc). In ch-2 sp work [4 dc, 1 ch, 4 dc], holding back last loop of each dc work 1 dc in each of second, third, and fourth dc (4 loops remain on hook), yarn over hook and pull through all 4 loops.
Row 4: Ch 1, turn, work 1 sc in fourth dc, ch 3, work 1 dc in each of next 2 dc (skip last dc), work 3 dc in ch-1 sp, holding back last loop of each dc work 1 dc in each of second, third, and fourth dc (4 loops remain on hook), yarn over hook and pull through all 4 loops.
Row 5: Ch 1, turn, work 1 sc in fourth dc, ch 3, holding back the last loop of each dc work 1 dc in each of next 2 dc (3 loops remain on hook), wrap yarn around hook and pull through all 3 loops. End of petal, fasten off.
Rep the above 5 rows in each ch-4 sp before beg the Lattice Work.

Connecting Lattice Work: Attach color B to the left side of any petal at the ch-1 st above the last dc of Petal Row 1.
Row 1: Ch 2, work 1 dc in the top of second dc of Rnd 4 (this will be the medallion below, and between two petals), ch 1, work 1 sc in top of ch 3 of second petal.
Row 2: Ch 3, work 1 sc in sc at beg of Petal Row 3 (on the right side of the second motif), ch 2, turn, work 1 dc in dc of row below (between the 2 petals), ch 2, work 1 sc in second dc at beg of Petal Row 3 (on first motif).
Row 3: Ch 3, work 1 sc in sc at beg of Petal Row 4 (of first motif), ch 3, turn, work [1 tr, ch 2, 1 tr] in dc of row below, ch 2, work 1 sc in above the ch 3 at beg of Petal Row 3 (on second motif).
Row 4: Ch 4, work 1 sc in the sc at beg of Petal Row 5 (on second motif), ch 3, turn, work [1 tr, ch 2, 1 tr, ch 2, 1 tr] in ch-2 sp of row below, work 1 tr in second dc at beg of Petal Row 4 (of first motif). Fasten off.
Rep Lattice Rows 1–4 between all petals.
Last Row of Lattice: Attach color B between the 2 dc sts of Petal Row 5 of any motif. **Ch 4, work 1 sc in tr sp of Lattice Row 4, ch 4, work 1 sc in

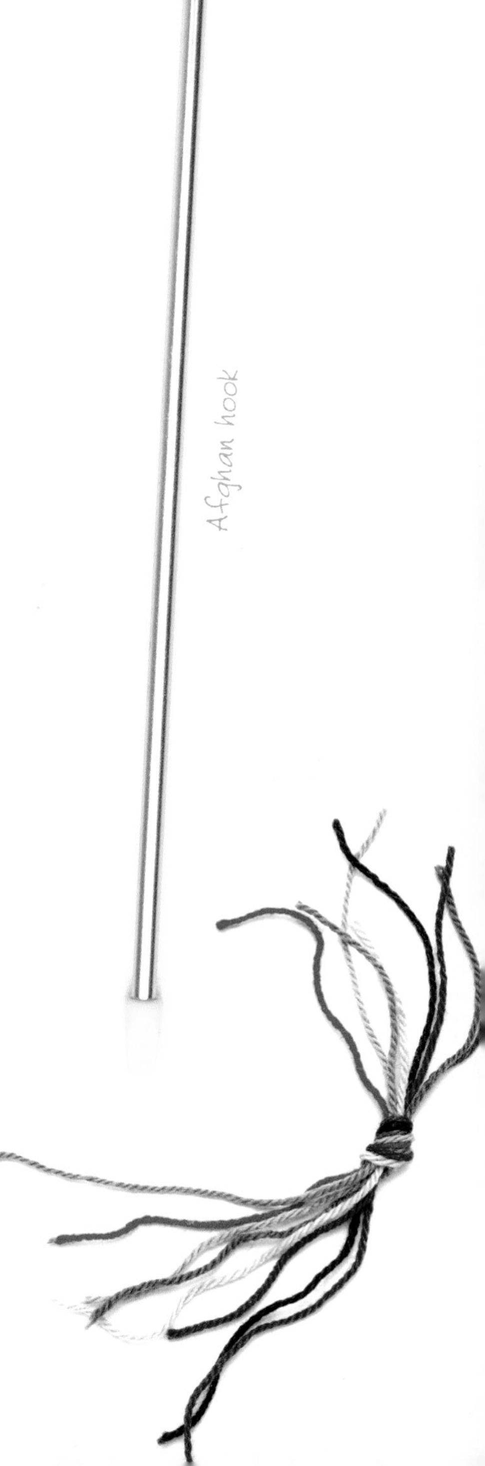

first ch-2 sp, ch 4, work 1 sc in next ch-2 sp, ch 4, work 1 sc in ch-3 sp, ch 4, work 1 sc between 2 dc of Petal Row 5, ch 4, work 1 ddc in tr sp of Lattice Row 4, ch 4, work [1 ddc, ch 4, 1 ddc] in first ch-2 sp, ch 8, work [1 ddc, ch 4, 1 ddc] in second ch-2 sp, ch 4, work 1 ddc in 3 ch, ch 4, work 1 sc between 2 dc of Petal Row 5**; rep from ** to ** 3 more times. Fasten off.

Double Crochet Round 1: Attach color G to any ch-8 sp, ch 3, work [2 dc, ch 2, 5 dc] in same sp, *work 3 dc in each of next 3 ch-4 sp, work 4 dc in next ch-4 sp, work 3 dc in each of next 4 ch-4 sp, work 4 dc in next ch-4 sp, work 3 dc in each of next 2 ch-4 sp, ** work [5 dc, ch 2, 5 dc] in ch-8 sp*; rep from * to * 2 more times, then from * to ** 1 time, end by working 2 dc in beg ch-8 sp. Join with sl st to top of ch 3. Fasten off.

Stripe Sequence: 2 rows navy (G), 4 rows purple (B), 2 rows dove (F), 4 rows aqua (A), 2 rows thistle (C), 2 rows charcoal (MC), 4 rows plum (D), 2 rows red (E).

Reverse Stripe Sequence: 2 rows red (E), 4 rows plum (D), 2 rows charcoal (MC), 2 rows thistle (C), 4 rows aqua (A), 2 rows dove (F), 4 rows purple (B), 2 rows navy (G).

BACK

Make the Motif first, following the above instructions. *With MC, working along one side of the motif and starting at a corner, ch 2, attach the yarn. (Review schematic for Back before starting.) Ch 3 (counts as 1 dc), work 1 dc in each dc and 1 dc in corner sp for a total of 47 dc. Turn, work even in dc for a total of 3½ (4½, 5½, 6½)" (9 [11.5, 14, 16.5] cm)*. Fasten off. Rep from * to * along opposite side edge of motif. ***Top Edge:*** With RS of work facing, join yarn to top of side piece and work 76 (82, 90, 98) dc evenly across the top edge of motif—these sts are distributed as follows: 14 (17, 21, 25) dc worked above the dc side stitches, 47 dc across the top edge of the motif, 15 (18, 22, 26) dc above remaining dc side stitches. Work even in dc across the 76 (82, 90, 98) dc for 3" (7.5 cm). Fasten off. ***Lower Back:*** With RS facing, attach MC at a corner of the motif bottom edge, ch 3 (counts as 1 dc) and work a total of 76 (82, 90, 98) stitches in dc along lower edge, sts should be spaced the same as the upper edge. Continuing in dc, work an additional 2 (4, 4, 6) rows in MC. Fasten off. Work the 22 rows as listed in the Reverse Stripe Sequence. End the back with 1 row dc in MC. Fasten off as follows: Cut yarn leaving 4" (10 cm) tail, thread tail through last lp on hook, pull to tighten and secure.

PLAIN BACK

(Alternative) Beg at lower edge with MC, ch 80 (86, 94, 102) sts. Insert hook in fifth ch from hook, and work 1 row in dc for a total of 76 (82, 90, 98) sts. Work 22 rows in Stripe Sequence, then change to MC and work even in dc until back measures 29 (30, 30, 31)" (73.5 [76, 76, 79] cm) from beg. Fasten off.

RIGHT FRONT

With MC ch 42 (46, 50, 54). Work 1 row dc starting with fifth ch from hook for a total of 38 (42, 46, 50) sts. Work in Stripe Sequence, then change back to MC and work even until work measures a total length of 21 (22, 22, 22)" (53.5 [56, 56, 56] cm) from beg, ending with a WS row. ***Shape Neck:*** (Work decreases by stopping 1 st short at the end of the row, or by working 1 sl st over the first st as the row begins). Begin shaping as follows: Dec 1 st at the end of the next row, and at the same edge every row 13 (14, 15, 16) more times. Work even on 24 (27, 30, 33) sts until right front measures 29 (30, 30, 31)" (73.5 [76, 76, 79] cm) from beg. Fasten off.

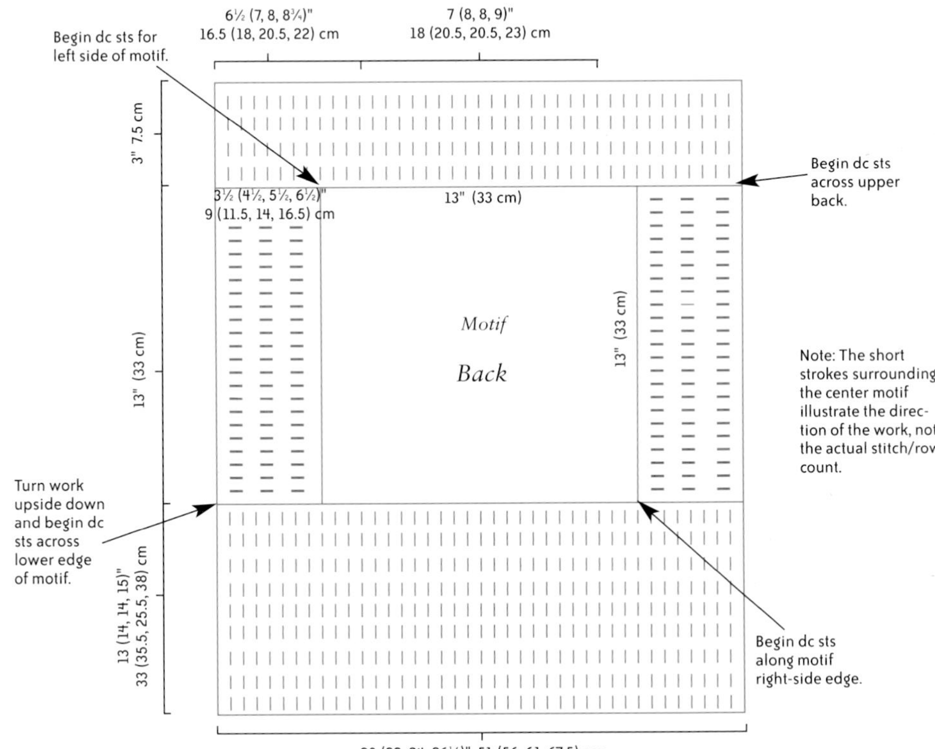

AFGHAN STITCH

Afghan stitch is also known as Tunisian crochet. In some ways it resembles knitting in both technique and resulting fabric. A special afghan hook is sized the same way as conventional crochet hooks, but it's longer and has a knob like a knitting needle opposite the hook. Instead of working one stitch at a time, use the afghan hook to pick up a loop in each stitch across the width of the work. Rows are worked in two parts; loops are first picked up across the row from right to left, then, without turning the work, yarn is wrapped around the hook and pulled through two loops at a time back across the row from left to right. The resulting fabric is fairly dense and distinctly different on each side, with a flat, smooth front and bumpy textured back that resembles stockinette stitch in knitting.

Afghan stitch is often used as a ground to embroider over, especially in cross-stitch embroidery, because the front side of the work sets up an even grid on which to place stitches. This feature provides an opportunity for colorful and detailed designs that would be much more complex to produce in crochet alone. To embroider on top of Afghan stitch, use contrast yarn to mark the center of the work for a centered design, or simply count stitches and rows to work a pattern. Work subsequent motifs counting from the embroidery already worked. Unlike embroidery on woven fabric, no hoops are used to keep Afghan-stitch fabric taut, so take care to make even stitches and do not pull too tightly. When you're starting a color, don't knot yarn on the back of work, but leave a tail of about 3" (7.5 cm) to work in later; also leave an ending tail to work in later.

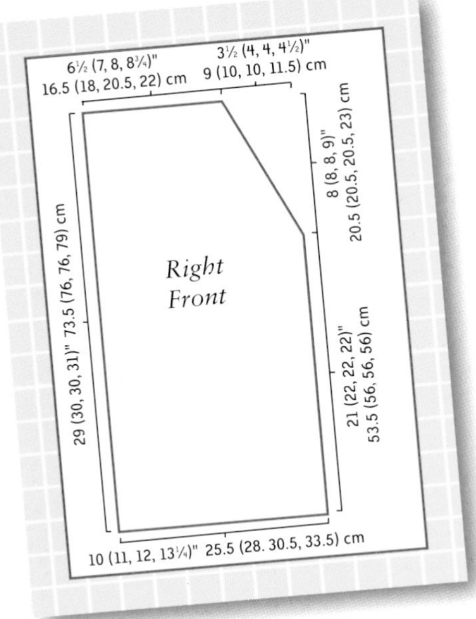

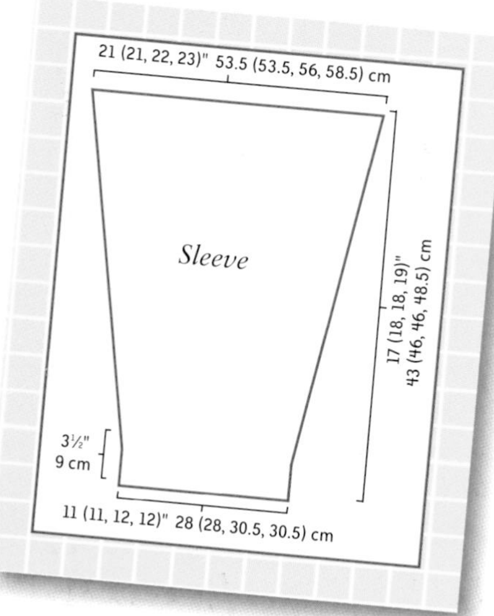

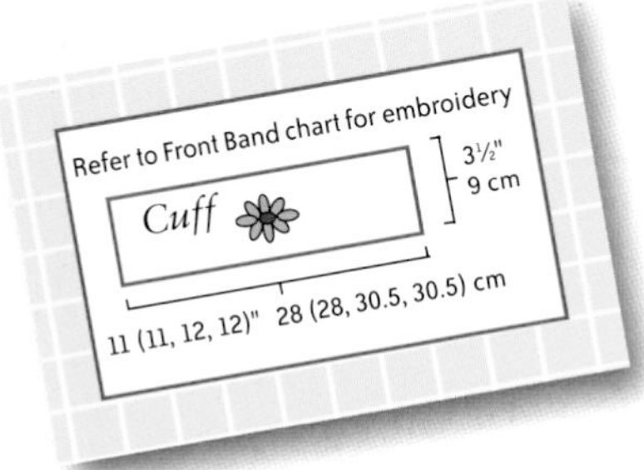

LEFT FRONT

Work same as Right Front, reversing neck shaping.

SLEEVES

(Make 2) With MC and hook, ch 43 (43, 47, 47) sts. *Next row:* Turn, ch 1, sc 42 (42, 46, 46) sts. Turn, ch 3 (counts as 1 dc), work 6 rows in dc. Work the following sleeve inc by working 1 dc in the same st as ch 3 at the beg of row, and working 2 dc in the last st of row. *Begin sleeve shaping:* Begin working Stripe Sequence colors and at the same time inc 6 (6, 6, 8) sts evenly across first row, then inc 1 st each edge every row 4 times, then every other row 11 (11, 11, 12) times for a total of 78 (78, 82, 86) sts. Change to MC when the 22-row Stripe Sequence has been completed. Work even in MC until sleeve measures 17 (18, 18, 19)" (43 [46, 46, 48.5] cm). Fasten off.

Cuffs: With afghan hook and MC, ch 15 sts. Work even in Basic Afghan Stitch to a total length of 11 (11, 12, 12)" (28 [28, 30.5, 30.5] cm). Fasten off. With crochet hook and MC, work Edging Stitch along 1 long edge. Fasten off. Mark the center of the cuff with contrast yarn. Work one Cross Stitch Flower Motif centered on cuff, using color C for petals and color E for center (see chart for the cross- stitch flower motif).

Front Band: With afghan hook and MC, ch 25 sts. Work in Basic Afghan Stitch for 266 (285, 285, 291) rows (parts 1 and 2) and a total length of about 66½ (71¼, 71¼, 72¾)" (168.5 [181, 181, 184.5] cm). Attach MC and work Edging Stitch along one long edge and both short edges at each end of band. Work the cross- stitch flowers along the band following the Flower Motif Chart.

FINISHING

Steam or block all pieces to size, especially the Afghan stitch pieces. With RS together, pin back and fronts together at shoulders. Slip-stitch crochet or backstitch shoulders together. To stabilize neck edge, slip-stitch crochet along back neck opening. With RS of cuff facing WS of sleeve, attach cuff to sleeve using backstitch or slip-stitch crochet. Mark center top of sleeve. Measure down 10½ (10½, 11, 11½)" (26.5 [26.5, 28, 29] cm) from shoulder seam on both front and back and mark with a pin. With RS together, pin sleeve to jacket matching center top of sleeve to shoulder seam and sleeve top edges to pin markers on body. Attach sleeve using either slip-stitch crochet or backstitch. With RS of work together, pin side and sleeve seams and seam in one using backstitch or slip-stitch crochet. Using backstitch, with RS together, stitch cuff seams. Pin front band to jacket with RS of band facing WS of jacket. Ease to fit as necessary. Using backstitch, sew in place. Fold band back to RS so that seam is covered. Tack bottom edge of band in place along lower edge of jacket. Remove pins.

Chart—Cross-Stitch Flower Motif for Front Band

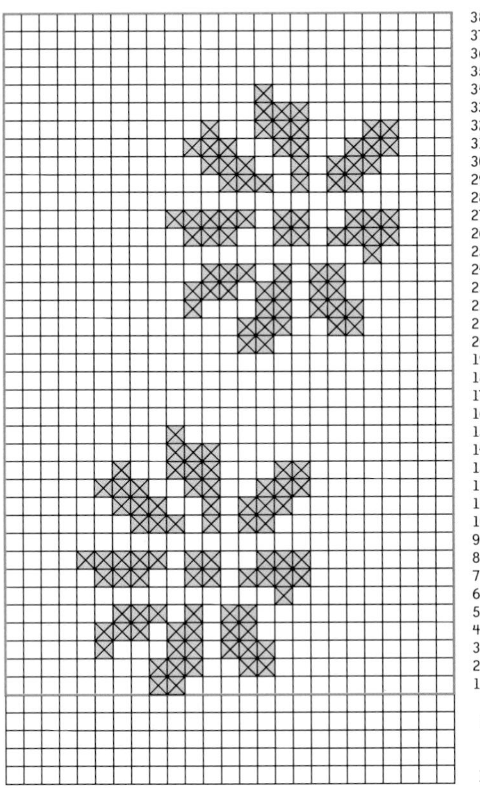

Small size: Beg first flower 3 rows above lower edge of Front Band. Repeat Rows 1–38 six times, then Rows 1–36 once—266 rows, 14 flowers. Embroider flowers using the colors as shown on the Front Band color sequence schematic.

Medium and Large sizes: Beg first flower 3 rows above the lower edge of Front Band. Repeat Rows 1–38 seven times, then work a single flower following Rows 1–15. After the final row 15, there should be 2 rows of Front Band remaining—285 rows, 15 flowers. Embroider flowers using the colors as shown on the Front Band color sequence schematic.

X-large size: Beg first flower on sixth row above lower edge of Front Band. Repeat Rows 1–38 seven times, then work Rows 1–15 once. After the final Row 15, there should be 5 rows of Front Band remaining—291 rows, 15 flowers. Embroider flowers using the colors as shown on the Front Band color sequence schematic.

Cross-stitching on Afghan Stitch

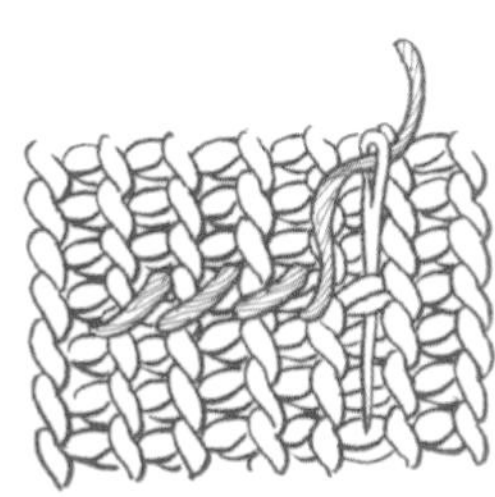

Work the first half of each stitch across the row following chart.

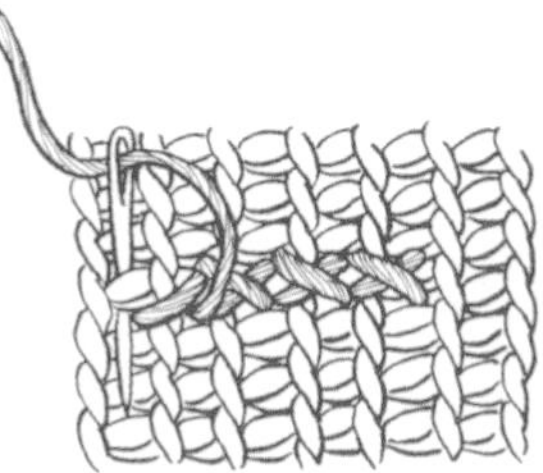

Finish the stitch coming back in the opposite direction.

Key for Cross-Stitch Flowers

A—#2346 aqua

B—#2395 purple

C—#2307 thistle

D—#2327 plum

E—#2358 red

F—#2303 dove

G—#2310 navy

Cross-stitch symbol, work in colors as shown in color placement chart, Front Band.

Front Band—color placement for cross-stitch flowers

S M, L, XL

E & C, D & F, G & E, C & A, B & F, D & G, C & B, E & C, A & D, F & E, D & A, C & F, A & G, F & B, E & C

6¼" 16 cm

66½ (71¼, 71¼, 72¾)" 168. 5 (181, 181, 184.5) cm

NESTED

BASKETS

Unclutter your surroundings and keep what you appreciate around you. These baskets are sturdy and flexible, so they're perfect to use on the table or floor. The trio fits one right inside another for easy storage when they're not in use.

SPECIFICATIONS

SIZE

Small Basket about 6" (15 cm) tall and 6" (15 cm) diameter; Medium Basket: about 9" (23 cm) tall and 9" (23 cm) diameter; Large Basket about 12" (30.5 cm) tall and 12" (30.5 cm) diameter.

YARN

Sportweight yarn, about 1350 yd (1234 m) of each color. ***We used:*** Louet Euroflax Linen (100% linen; 270 yd [247 m]/100 g): 5 skeins each color #3364 natural (A) and #2504 sage (B).

HOOK

Size E/4 (3.5mm). Adjust hook size if necessary to obtain correct gauge.

NOTIONS

Tapestry needle.

GAUGE

24 stitches and 20 rounds = 4" (10 cm) in circular single crochet with two strands of yarn together with size E/4 (3.5 mm) hook.

linen creates a good, sturdy basket

ABBREVIATIONS

ch—chain
lp(s)—loop(s)
rep—repeat
rnd—round(s)
sc—single crochet
sl st—slip stitch
st(s)—stitch(es)

Review Basics, page 2:
Chain
Increasing
Reading a pattern
Single crochet
Slip stitch
Weaving in ends

SMALL BASKET

With hook and 2 strands of color A held together throughout, ch 4 sts. Join into a ring as follows (see page 23): Insert hook into first ch and join with sl st to lp on hook.

Rnd 1: Ch 1, work 8 sc in ring, join with sl st to ch—8 sts.

Rnd 2: Ch 1, work 2 sc in each sc, join with sl st to ch—16 sts.

Rnd 3: Ch 1, *work 1 sc in first sc, work 2 sc in next sc*; rep from * to * around, join with sl st to ch—24 sts.

Rnd 4: Ch 1, *work 1 sc in first sc, work 2 sc in next sc*; rep from * to * around, join with sl st to ch—36 sts.

Rnd 5: Ch 1, *work 1 sc in each of first 2 sc, work 2 sc in next sc*; rep from * to * around, join with sl st to ch—48 sts.

Rnd 6: Ch 1, work even in sc, join with sl st to ch.

Rnd 7: Ch 1, *work 1 sc in each of first 3 sc, work 2 sc in next sc*; rep from * to * around, join with sl st to ch—60 sts.

Rnd 8: Ch 1, work even in sc, join with sl st to ch.
Rnd 9: Ch 1, *work 1 sc in each of first 4 sc, work 2 sc in next sc*; rep from * to * around, join with sl st to ch—72 sts.
Rnd 10: Ch 1, work even in sc, join with sl st to ch.
Rnd 11: Ch 1, *work 1 sc in each of first 5 sc, work 2 sc in next sc*; rep from * to * around, join with sl st to ch—84 sts.
Rnd 12: Ch 1, work even in sc, join with sl st to ch.
Rnd 13: Ch 1, *work 1 sc in each of first 6 sc, work 2 sc in next sc*; rep from * to * around, join with sl st to ch—96 sts.
Rnds 14–15: Ch 1, work even in sc, join with sl st to ch.
Note: The next round is the turning round, and will form a ridge that changes the work from the base to form the wall of the basket side.
Rnd 16: Ch 1, working *the outside half only of each sc stitch* (see page 101) work to end of rnd, sl st to ch.

Basket Side
Rnds 17–20: Continue with color A, ch 1, and resume working sc as before, inserting hook under both halves of the st, to the end of the rnd, join with sl st to ch. Fasten off both yarns as follows: Cut yarn leaving 4" (10 cm) tail, insert tail through last lp on hook and pull to tighten.
Rnds 21–24: Join color B, ch 1, work sc to the end of the rnd, join with sl st to ch. Fasten off.
Rnds 25–28: Rep Rnds 17–20.
Rnds 29–32: Rep Rnds 21–24.
Rnds 33–36: Rep Rnds 17–20.
Rnds 37–40: Rep Rnds 21–24.
Rnds 41–44: Rep Rnds 17–20.
Rnds 45–48: Rep Rnds 21–24.

MEDIUM BASKET

With hook and 2 strands of color B held together throughout, ch 4 sts. Join into a ring as follows (see page 23): Insert hook into first ch and join with sl st to lp on hook. With color B, work same as for Small Basket through Rnd 14.
Rnd 15: Ch 1, *work 1 sc in each of first 7 sc, work 2 sc in next sc*; rep from * to * to end of rnd, join with sl st to ch—108 sts.
Rnd 16: Ch 1, work even in sc, join with sl st to ch.
Rnd 17: Ch 1, *work 1 sc in each of first 8 sc, work 2 sc in next sc*; rep from * to * to end of rnd, join with sl st to ch—120 sts.
Rnd 18: Ch 1, work even in sc, join with sl st to ch.
Rnd 19: Ch 1, *work 1 sc in each of first 9 sc, work 2 sc in next sc*; rep from * to * to end of rnd, join with sl st to ch—132 sts.
Rnd 20: Ch 1, work even in sc, join with sl st to ch.
Rnd 21: Ch 1, * work 1 sc in each of first 10 sc, work 2 sc in next sc*; rep from * to * around, join with sl st to ch—144 sts.

Rnd 22: Ch 1, work even, join with sl st to ch. Fasten off as follows: Cut yarn leaving 4" (10 cm) tail, insert tail through last lp on hook and pull to tighten

Rnd 23: Attach color A, ch 1, work turning rnd same as Rnd 16 of Small Basket, join with sl st to ch.

Rnds 24–41: With color A, ch 1, resume working sc through both halves of st, to end of rnd, join with sl st to ch. Fasten off as follows: Cut yarn leaving 4" (10 cm) tail, insert tail through last lp on hook and pull to tighten.

Rnds 42–52: With color B, ch 1, work sc to end of rnd, join with sl st to ch. Fasten off.

Rnds 53–70: With color A, ch 1, work sc to end of rnd, join with sl st to ch. Fasten off.

LARGE BASKET

With hook and 2 strands of color A held together throughout, ch 4 sts. Join into a ring as follows (see page 23): Insert hook into first ch and join with sl st to lp on hook. With color A, work same as for Medium Basket through Rnd 22—144 sts. Don't fasten off yarn.

Rnd 23: Ch 1, work 1 sc in each of first 11 sc, work 2 sc in next sc*; rep from * to * to end of rnd, join with sl st to ch—156 sts.

Rnds 24–25: Ch 1, work even in sc, join with sl st to ch.

Rnd 26: Ch 1, *work 1 sc in each of next 12 sc, work 2 sc in next sc*; rep from * to * to end of rnd, join with sl st to ch—168 sts.

Rnds 27–28: Ch 1, work even in sc, join with sl st to ch.

Rnd 29: Ch 1, work 1 sc in each of first 13 sc, work 2 sc in next sc*; rep from * to * around, join with sl st to ch—180 sts.

Rnds 30–31: Ch 1, work even in sc, join with sl st to ch. Fasten off color A.

Rnd 32: Change to color B and work turning rnd same as Rnd 16 of Small Basket.

Rnds 33–44: Continue with color B, ch 1, resume sc as before (working through both halves of each sc) to end of rnd, join with sl st to ch.

Rnds 45–56: Join A, ch 1, work in sc to end of rnd, join with sl st to ch.

Rnds 57–68: Rep Rnds 33–44.

Rnds 69–80: Rep Rnds 45–56.

Rnds 81–92: Rep Rnds 33–44.

FINISHING

With tapestry needle, work in all loose yarn ends to wrong side, and trim close to work. Fold the top edge down about 1" (2.5 cm) for small and medium baskets and 2" (5 cm) for large basket to form a rim around the top.

PERPENDICULAR CROCHET

When you're working in rounds, say for a hat or bag, the general technique is to increase from the base to the desired diameter, then to work even without any increasing. After a few rounds of working even without increases, the piece curves gradually and begins to form a cylindrical shape. When you want a clean, sharp edge instead of a gradual curve, you can make a few manipulations of simple stitches to work perpendicular crochet.

The basic principle of perpendicular crochet involves working into half a stitch either the front or back. Whether you use the inside or outside half of the stitch influences the direction that the fabric turns. When you work into half a stitch on just one well-placed round (in the case of the Nested Baskets, the well-placed round was where the corners angled), it gives the effect of a mitered corner in which the two rounds meet at an angle. In some cases, especially when you want a firm shape, work one round of slip-stitch crochet in the first round, then half the slip stitch on the following round.

worked flat

worked circular

ORGANIC BASKETS

Reminiscent of rocks, maybe even potatoes, these "lumpy" baskets prove that symmetry isn't everything. Free-form crochet can create almost any sculptural form imaginable. Here, just for fun, the baskets use unbalanced increases and decreases, and the protuberances can be pushed in or out as desired.

You can sculpt a face using free-form crochet

SPECIFICATIONS

SIZE

Small Basket: 5" (12.5 cm) tall, 5½" (14 cm) in diameter; Large Basket: 7" (18 cm) tall, 7" (18 cm) in diameter.

YARN

Super bulky-weight wool. About 132 yd [121 m] for small basket and 264 yd [241 m] for large basket. ***We used:*** Brown Sheep's Burly Spun (100% wool, 132 yd [121 m]/226 g): 1 skein BS-03 grey heather (A) and BS-06 deep charcoal (C), 2 skeins each BS-04 charcoal heather (B).

HOOK

Size K/10½ (6.5 mm). Adjust hook size if necessary to obtain the correct gauge.

NOTIONS

Tapestry needle (optional); large safety pin or paper clip for marking rounds.

GAUGE

10 stitches and 11 rounds = 4" (10 cm) worked in circular single crochet with size K/10½ (6.5 mm) hook.

ABBREVIATIONS

ch—chain
dec—decrease(ing)
inc—increase(ing)
lp—loop
rep—repeat
sc—single crochet
sc2tog—sc 2 stitches together (see following note)
sl st—slip stitch
st(s)—stitch(es)

Review Basics, page 2:
Chain stitch
Increasing
Joining colors
Reading a pattern
Single crochet
Slip stitch
Weaving in ends
Working in rounds

Note: Unlike previous patterns worked in the round, the rounds on these baskets are not joined with a slip stitch, but are worked in a continuous spiral technique (see page 23). To make the increases, simply work two single crochet into one single crochet stitch. To work decreases (sc2tog) insert hook in first single crochet and pull up a loop (2 loops on hook), insert hook into next single crochet and pull up another loop (3 loops on hook), wrap yarn around hook, and pull through all three loops on hook.

SMALL BASKET

With color A and hook, ch 3 sts, join with sl st to form ring (see page 23).
Rnd 1: Work 8 sc into the ring, mark the end stitch with a safety pin or paper clip (move this marker to the end stitch after each round).
Rnd 2: Work 2 sc in each sc to end of rnd—16 sts.
Rnd 3: *Work 1 sc in the first sc, work 2 sc in next sc*: rep from * to * to end of rnd—24 sts.

FREE-FORM CROCHET

Crochet is the perfect medium for creating sculptural forms in fiber. Because each stitch is a unit unto itself, crochet can go in any direction—forward, backward, up or down—without affecting the work already created. You can therefore form any imaginable shape. By using a hook that's small in relation to the weight of the yarn, and by working in single crochet—which makes the firmest, most dense fabric of all the crochet stitches—you can create a fabric whose rigidity further emphasizes the sculptural form.

The most basic way to experiment with free-form crochet is to play with the placement of increases and decreases. Conventionally they are evenly placed. In free-form crochet, increases concentrated in one area push that area forward. Conversely, concentrated decreases pull in an area. To further enhance an organic form, turn the work around at any juncture to create more rows in one area than on the rest of the form. These areas are known as short rows. To integrate them into the form smoothly, work a slip stitch at the turning point. You can also use slip stitches to move along certain areas without adding the height of another row or round, or to work across the surface in any direction. The slip stitches can then act as a foundation for other stitches. Changing color at strategic points can further emphasize form.

When you have mastered the basics of crochet and want to get creative with the technique, free-form crochet opens up a whole new third dimension.

Rnd 4: *Work 1 sc in each of first 2 sc, work 2 sc in next sc*; rep from * to * to end of rnd—32 sts.
Note: From this point on the increases and decreases are occurring on an irregular basis. Stitch count will not stay constant; therefore keeping track of the end of each round by moving the marker is very important.
Rnd 5: Work 1 sc in each of first 3 sc, *work 2 sc in next sc, work 1 sc in next sc*; rep from * to * 7 more times. Work 1 sc in each of next 13 sc—40 sts.
Rnd 6: *Work 1 sc in each of first 4 sc, work 2 sc in each of next 4 sc*; rep from * to * 1 more time, work 1 sc in each of next 24 sc—48 sts.
Rnds 7 and 8: Work even.
Rnd 9: Work 1 sc in each of next 8 sc, sc2tog, work 1 sc in each of next 4 sc, sc2tog 4 times, work 1 sc in each of next 12 sc, work 2 sc in each of next 6 sc, work 1 sc in each of next 8 sc—49 sts.
Rnd 10: Work 1 sc in each of next 6 sc, sc2tog 2 times, work 1 sc in next 6 sc, sc2tog, work 1 sc in next sc, sc2tog 2 times, work 1 sc in next 4 sc, (work 2 sc in next sc, 1sc in next sc) 4 times, work 1 sc in each of next 6 sc, work 2 sc in each of next 4 sc, work 1 sc in each of next 4 sc—52 sts.
Rnd 11: Work 1 sc in each of first 13 sc, sc2tog, work 1 sc in next sc, sc2tog, work 1 sc in each of next 22 sc, (work 2 sc in next sc, 1 sc in next sc) 4 times, work 1 sc in each of next 4 sc—54 sts.
Rnd 12: Work even.
Rnd 13: Work 1 sc in each of first 9 sc, (sc2tog, work 1 sc in next sc) 3 times, work 1 sc in each of next 4 sc, (sc2tog, work 1 sc in next sc) 3 times, work 1 sc in each of next 12 sc, sc2tog 4 times, work 1 sc in next 3 sc—44 sts.
Rnd 14: Work even.
Rnd 15: Work 1 sc in each of next 23 sc, sc2tog, work 1 sc in each of next 6 sc, sc2tog, work 1 sc in each of next 5 sc, sc2tog, work 1 sc in each of next 4 sc—41 sts.
Rnd 16: Work 1 sc in each of next 38 sc, sc2tog, 1 sc—40 sts.
Rnd 17: Work even, working sl st into last st to join rnd. Fasten off as follows: Cut yarn leaving 4" (10 cm) tail, insert tail through last lp on hook and pull to tighten.
Rnd 18: Attach color B, ch 1, work even in sc, join with sl st to ch 1. Fasten off.

■ LARGE BASKET

Using color B, work the same as for Small Basket through Rnd 4—32 sts.
Rnd 5: *Work 1 sc in each of next 3 sc, work 2 sc in next sc*; rep from * to * to end of rnd—40 sts.
Rnd 6: *Work 1 sc in each of next 4 sc, work 2 sc in next sc*; rep from * to * to end of rnd—48 sts.
Rnd 7: *Work 1 sc in each of next 5 sc, work 2 sc in next sc*; rep from * to * to end of rnd—56 sts.
Rnd 8: Work even.
Rnd 9: *Work 1 sc in each of first 6 sc, work 2 sc in next sc*; rep from * to * to end of rnd—64 sts.

Rnds 10 and 11: Work even.
Rnd 12: Work 1 sc in each of first 10 sc, (work 2 sc in next sc, 1 sc in next sc) 4 times, work 1 sc in each of next 16 sc, (work 2 sc in next sc, 1 sc in next sc) 3 times, work 1 sc in each of next 12 sc, (work 2 sc in next sc, 1 sc in next sc) 2 times, work 1 sc in each of next 8 sc—73 sts.
Rnd 13: Work 1 sc in each of next 16 sc, work 2 sc in each of next 4 sc, work 1 sc in each of next 18 sc, (work 2 sc in next sc, 1 sc in next sc) 3 times, work 1 sc in each of next 16 sc, (work 2 sc in next sc, 1 sc in next sc) 3 times, work 1 sc in each of next 7 sc—83 sts.
Rnd 14: Work even.
Rnd 15: Work 1 sc in each of next 18 sc, (sc2 tog, 1 sc in next sc) 4 times, work 1 sc in each of next 14 sc, (sc2tog, 1 sc in next sc) 4 times, work 1 sc in each of next 16 sc, (sc2tog, 1 sc in next sc) 3 times, sc in next 2 st—72 sts.
Rnd 16: Work even.
Rnd 17: Work 1 sc in each of next 16 sc, sc2tog, work 1 sc in each of next 3 sc, sc2tog, work 1 sc in next sc, sc2tog, work 1 sc in each of next 4 sc, sc2tog, work 1 sc in each of next 10 sc, (sc2tog, 1 sc in next sc) 2 times, work 1 sc in each of next 10 sc, sc2tog, work 1 sc in each of next 2 sc, sc2tog, work 1 sc in each of next 8 sc—64 sts.
Rnd 18: Work even.
Rnd 19: Work 1 sc in each of next 6 sc, (work 2 sc in next sc, 1 sc in next sc) 4 times, work 1 sc in each of next 12 sc, (work 2 sc in next sc, 1 sc in next sc) 3 times, work 1 sc in each of next 14 sc, (work 2 sc in next sc, 1 sc in next sc) 3 times, work 1 sc in each of next 12 sc—74 sts.
Rnd 20: Work 1 sc in each of next 8 sc, (work 2 sc in next sc, 1 sc in next sc) 3 times, work 1 sc in each of next 18 sc, (work 2 sc in next sc, 1 sc in next sc) 4 times, work 1 sc in each of next 14 sc, (work 2 sc in next sc, 1 sc in next sc) 3 times, work 1 sc in each of next 14 sc—84 sts.
Rnd 21: Work even.
Rnd 22: Work 1 sc in each of next 8 sc, (sc2tog, 1 sc in next sc) 3 times, work 1 sc in each of next 16 sc, (sc2tog, 1 sc in next sc) 4 times, work 1 sc in each of next 12 sc, (sc2tog, 1 sc in next sc) 3 times, work 1 sc in each of next 18 sc—74 sts.
Rnd 23: Work even.
Rnd 24: Work 1 sc in each of next 10 sc, sc2tog, work 1 sc in each of next 16 sc, (sc2tog, 1 sc in next sc) 2 times, work 1 sc in each of next 6 sc, sc2tog, work 1 sc in next 11 sc, (sc2tog, work 1 sc in next sc) 2 times, work 1 sc in each of next 15 sc—68 sts.
Rnd 25: Work even.
Rnd 26: Work 1 sc in each of next 8 sc, sc2tog, work 1 sc in next sc, sc2tog, work 1 sc in each of next 4 sc, sc2tog, work 1 sc in each of next 10 sc, sc2tog, work 1 sc in each of next 18 sc, sc2tog, work 1 sc in each of next 10 sc, sc2tog, work 1 sc in each of next 5 sc—62 sts.
Rnd 27: Work 1 sc in each of next 8 sc, sc2tog, work 1 sc in next sc, sc2tog, work 1 sc in each of next 14 sc, sc2tog, work 1 sc in each of next 16 sc, sc2tog, work 1 sc in each of next 7 sc, sc2tog, work 1 sc in each of next 6 sc—57 sts.
Rnd 28: Work even.
Rnd 29: Work even, working sl st into last st to join. Fasten off as follows: Cut yarn leaving 4" (10 cm) tail, insert tail through last lp on hook and pull to tighten.
Rnd 30: Attach color C, ch 1, 57 sc, join with sl st to ch 1. Fasten off.

CHAOTIC BOBBLE

PILLOW

This pillow plays with bobbles and can be arranged in different configurations—neat and orderly, rows of stripes, or popping out all over each other.

SPECIFICATIONS

SIZE

About 14" (35.5 cm) square. *Important Note:* In order for pillow to cover pillow forms smoothly, the crocheted covers should be *slightly smaller than the pillow form*. The pillow cover, before stuffing, should measure about 13½" (34.5 cm) square.

YARN

Worsted-weight yarn, about 500 yd (458 m). ***We used:*** Jo Sharp Silkroad Tweed (85% wool, 10% silk, 5% cashmere; 104 yd [95 m]/50 g): 6 balls: #121, brindle. About 10 yd (9 m) contrasting yarn of similar weight for crocheting edges together.

HOOK

Size H/8 (5 mm). Adjust hook size if necessary to obtain the correct gauge.

NOTIONS

14" (35.5 cm) square pillow form; 3 buttons, about 1" (3.2 cm) in diameter; tapestry needle; straight pins; safety pins to mark button placements.

GAUGE

Pillow front: 15 sts = 4½" (11.5 cm); 12½ rows = 4" (10 cm) in Honeycomb Stitch with size H/8 (5 mm) hook. Pillow back: 10 sts = 3" (7.5 cm); 12 rows = 5" (12.5 cm) in half double crochet with size H/8 (5 mm) hook.

ABBREVIATIONS

beg—begin(s), beginning
ch(s)—chain(s)
hdc—half double crochet
lp(s)—loop(s)
rep—repeat
sc—single crochet
sk—skip
st(s)—stitch(es)
yo—yarn over

Review Basics, page 2:
Chain stitch
Half double crochet
Reading a pattern
Seaming
Single crochet
Slip stitch
Weaving in ends

PATTERN STITCH

Honeycomb Stitch Pattern

Make a foundation ch of a multiple of 3 sts + 2 edge sts and 1 turning chain. Work 1 row sc. Ch 1, turn work.

Row 1: Work 1 sc (edge stitch), *yo, insert hook in next st, (yo, draw up lp, yo, draw through first 2 lps on hook) 5 times, yo, draw through all 6 lps on hook, work 1 sc in each of next 2 sts*; rep from * to * across row, end with 1 sc (edge stitch). Ch 1, turn.

Row 2: Work 1 sc in each st. Ch 1, turn.

Row 3: Work 1 sc in first st (edge stitch), *work 1 sc in each of next 2 sts, yo, insert hook into next st (yo, draw up lp, yo, draw through first 2 lps on hook) 5 times, yo, draw through all 6 lps on hook*; rep from * to * across row, end with 1 sc in last st (edge stitch).
Row 4: Rep Row 2.
Rep Rows 1–4 for pattern.

PILLOW TOP

With yarn and hook, loosely ch 48 sts. Beg in second ch from hook, work 1 sc in each ch—47 sts. Ch 1, turn. Work in Honeycomb Stitch pattern to a total length of 13½" (34.5 cm) in length from beg ch, ending with either Row 2 or Row 4. Work one more row in sc. Fasten off as follows: Cut yarn leaving 4" (10 cm) tail, insert tail through last lp on hook and pull to tighten.

PILLOW BACK

Upper Portion: With yarn and hook, loosely ch 48 sts. Beg in second ch from hook, work 1 row sc in each ch—47 sts. Ch 2, turn. Work 1 row hdc beg in third ch from hook—47 sts. Ch 2, turn. *Buttonhole Row:* (see page 71) hdc in each of first 6 sts, *ch 3, sk next 3 hdc, work 1 hdc in each of next 13 sts*; rep from * to * once more, ch 3, sk next 3 sts, 1 hdc in each of last 6 hdc. Continue working in hdc until piece measures a total length of 5¼" (13.5 cm) from beg ch. Turn, ch 1, work 1 row sc. Fasten off.
Bobble Edge: With right side of work facing, attach yarn to side edge of beg ch. Work Row 1 of Honeycomb Pattern. Fasten off.
Lower Portion: With yarn and hook, loosely ch 49 sts. Beg in third ch from hook, work 47 hdc. Ch 2, turn. Work in hdc to a total length of 10" (25.5 cm). Fasten off.

FINISHING

With threaded tapestry needle, work in loose ends to wrong side of work and weave through several sts to secure. Lightly steam and block pieces to size. With wrong sides together, pin pillow top to back, overlapping upper back piece over lower back piece to fit size of front. With contrast yarn, beg at a corner, work slip-stitch crochet evenly around entire edge close to edge. Fasten off. Mark directly under buttonholes by placing safety pins through the buttonholes onto the underside where the buttons will be sewn. With threaded tapestry needle, sew buttons at markers. Remove all pins. Insert pillow form and fluff to fill out pillow.

RAISED STITCHES

Clusters, bobbles, popcorns, and puff stitches all add texture to the surface of crocheted fabric. To form any of these stitches, work several stitches into one stitch, then join the group of stitches together at the top. The joining forces the group forward to sit above the body of the work while it keeps the stitch count constant.

In a popcorn stitch, after several double or treble crochet stitches are worked into one stitch, the hook is removed from the stitch, reinserted into the top of the first stitch of the cluster, and then back into the working loop. The stitches are then worked together to close up the popcorn. In bobble stitches and puff stitches, several stitches are worked into one stitch but the stitches are not completed until the last loop is drawn through all the loops on the hook. Cluster stitches follow the same principle except that the elongated stitches, at least half double crochet, but more often double crochet or even treble crochet, are worked into adjacent stitches and then joined together at the top. In some instances, cluster stitches are worked into the stitch a row or two directly below what would normally be the next stitch.

OPULENT

PILLOW

No need for a commonplace pillow when you can use a variety of novelty yarns. Novelties dress up simple stitches and stitch combinations, and the pillow is a great way to use up leftovers.

SPECIFICATIONS

SIZE

17" (43 cm) square to fit snugly on an 18" (46 cm) pillow form.

YARN

About 900 yds (830 m) worsted-weight novelty yarns. ***We used:*** Berroco Cotton Twist (70% mercerized cotton, 30% rayon; 85 yd [78 m]/50 g) 2 skeins each #8353 organic teal (B), #8316 blue gabardine (C), 1 skein #8362 parlor (G); Softwist (41% wool, 59% rayon; 100 yd [92 m]/50 g) 1 skein each #9439 ginger (H), #9478 garnet (E); Jewel FX (94% rayon, 6% metallic; 57 yd [52 m]/25 g) 1 skein #6902 mother of pearl (D); Metallic FX (85% rayon, 15% metallic; 85 yd [78 m]/25 g]) 1 skein #1001 gold (I); Quest (100% nylon; 82 yd [76 m] /50 g]) 1 skein each #9813 rose glow (A), #9812 copper (F).

HOOK

Size H/8 (5mm). Adjust hook size if necessary to obtain the correct gauge.

NOTIONS

Three buttons, about 1" (2.5 cm) in diameter, one pillow form 18" (46 cm) square; tapestry needle, long sewing pins with large colored heads; sewing needle; button thread to attach buttons.

GAUGE

16 stitches and 16 rows = 4" (10 cm) in single crochet with size H/8 (5 mm) hook, worked in a sample using several of the yarns.

Consider making the front and back the same

ABBREVIATIONS

beg—begin(ning)
ch—chain
dc—double crochet
dctog cluster—4 or 5 double crochet stitches worked together as one to form a cluster
hdc—half double crochet
lp(s)—loop(s)
rep—repeat
rnd(s)—round(s)
sc—single crochet
sk—skip
sl—slip
sl st—slip st
sp—space
st(s)—stitch(es)

lots of textures to choose from

Review Basics, page 2:
Chain stitch
Double crochet
Half double crochet
Joining yarns
Reading a pattern
Single crochet
Seaming
Weaving in ends

PILLOW FRONT

With hook and yarn D, ch 4 sts, join with sl st to form a ring (see page 6).
Rnd 1: Ch 3 (counts as 1 dc), work 11 dc into ring—12 sts. Join rnd to top of ch 3.
Rnd 2: Ch 3, work 4dctog cluster in same st, work 1 hdc in next st, work 1 5dctog cluster, ch 4, *work (1 5dctog in next st, 1hdc in next st, 1 5dctog in next) ch 4*; rep from * to * 2 more times. Join rnd with sl st to top of ch 3. Fasten off as follows: Cut yarn leaving 4" (10 cm) tail, insert tail through last lp on hook and pull to tighten.
Rnd 3: Attach yarn B in any ch-4 sp. Ch 2 (counts as 1 hdc) work (2 hdc, 2 ch, 3hdc) in same sp, work 1 hdc in each of next 3 sts, *in ch-4 sp work (3hdc, 2 ch, 3hdc), work 1 hdc in each of next 3 sts*; rep from * to * 2 more times. Join rnd with sl st to top of beg ch. Fasten off.
Rnd 4: Attach yarn A in any ch-2 sp. Ch 3 (counts as 1 dc), work (2 dc, 2 ch, 3 dc) in same sp, *work 1 dc in each of next 9 sts, in corner sp work (3 dc, 2 ch, 3 dc)*; rep from * to * 2 more times. Join rnd with sl st to top of ch 3. Fasten off.
Rnd 5: Attach yarn B in any ch-2 sp. Ch 2 (counts as 1 hdc) work (1 hdc, 3 ch, 2 hdc) in same sp, *work 1 hdc in each of next 15 sts, work (2 hdc, 3 ch, 2 hdc) in ch-2 sp*; rep from * to * 2 more times. Join rnd with sl st to top of beg ch 2. Fasten off.
Rnd 6: Attach yarn C in any ch-3 sp. Ch 2 (counts as 1 hdc), work (1 hdc, 3 ch, 2

hdc) in same sp, *skip next st, work 2 hdc in next st*; rep from * to * to next ch 3 sp. In ch-3 sp work (2 hdc, ch 3, 2 hdc)**; rep from * to ** 2 more times, then rep from * to * 1 more time. Join rnd with sl st to top of beg ch. Fasten off.
Rnd 7: Attach yarn D in any ch-3 sp. Ch 3 (counts as 1 dc) work (1 dc, ch 3, 2 dc) in same sp. Work 1 dc in each of next 22 hdc, *work (2 dc, 3 ch, 2 dc) in ch-3 sp, work 1 dc in each of next 22 hdc*; rep from * to * 2 more times. Join rnd with sl st to beg ch 3.
Rnd 8: Attach yarn B in any ch-3 sp. Work same as Rnd 6. Join rnd to top of beg ch. Fasten off.
Rnd 9: Attach yarn E in any ch-3 sp. Work same as Rnd 6. Join rnd to top of beg ch. Fasten off.
Rnd 10: Attach yarn F in any ch-3 sp. Work same as Rnd 6. Join rnd to top of beg ch. Fasten off.
Rnd 11: Attach yarn C in any ch-3 sp. Work same as Rnd 6. Join rnd to top of beg ch. Fasten off.
Rnd 12: Attach yarn G in any ch-3 sp. Work same as Rnd 6. Join rnd to top of beg ch. Fasten off.
Rnd 13: Attach yarn H in any ch-3 sp. Work same as Rnd 6. Join rnd to top of beg ch. Fasten off.
Rnd 14: Attach yarn E in any ch-3 sp. Work same as Rnd 6. Join rnd to top of beg ch. Fasten off.
Rnd 15: Attach yarn A in any ch-3 sp. Ch 2 (counts as 1 hdc), work (1 hdc, 3 ch, 2 hdc) in same sp, work 1 hdc in first st. Work 4dctog cluster in next st, *work 1 hdc in each of next 2 sts, work 4 hdc cluster in next st*; rep from * to * to corner, work (2 hdc, 3 ch, 2 hdc) in corner.** Rep from * to ** 2 more times, then rep from * to *. Join rnd to top of beg ch with sl st. Fasten off.
Rnd 16: Attach yarn C in any ch-3 sp. Ch 2 (counts as 1 hdc), work (1 hdc, 3 ch, 2 hdc) in same sp, work 1 hdc in each of first 3 sts, *work 1 sc above cluster, work 1 hdc in each of next 2 sts*; rep from * to * to corner, work (2 hdc, 3 ch, 2 hdc) in corner**; rep from * to ** 2 more times, then rep from * to *. Join rnd with sl st to top of beg ch. Fasten off.
Rnd 17: Attach yarn I in any ch-3 sp. Work same as Rnd 7. Join rnd with sl st to top of beg ch. Fasten off.
Rnd 18: Attach yarn B in any ch-3 sp. Work same as Rnd 6. Join rnd with sl st to top of beg ch. Fasten off.
Rnd 19: Attach yarn D in any ch-3 sp. Work same as Rnd 7. Join rnd with sl st to top of beg ch. Fasten off.
Rnd 20: Attach yarn C in any ch-3 sp. Work same as Rnd 6. Join rnd with sl st to top of beg ch. Fasten off.

■ PILLOW BACK

Top Portion: With hook and yarn C, ch 67 sts. Work 1 row sc—66sts. Turn work. Fasten off.
Row 2: Attach yarn D, ch 3 (counts as 1 dc), starting with fifth ch from hook, work 1 dc in each st across row—66 sts. Turn work. Fasten off.
Row 3: Attach yarn B. Ch 1, work 1 sc in each st. Turn.

Row 4: (buttonhole row) Ch 1, work 1 sc in each of first 9 sts, *ch 3, sk next 3 sts, work 1 sc in each of next 19 sts*; rep from * to * once, ch 3, sk next 3 sts, work 1 sc in each of last 10 sts (3 buttonholes). Turn. Fasten off.
Row 5: Attach yarn E. Ch 2, work 1 hdc in same st, *sk next st, work 2 hdc in next st.* Rep from * to * across row. Turn. Fasten off.
Row 6: Attach yarn F, work same as Row 5.
Row 7: Attach yarn C, work same as Row 5.
Row 8: Attach yarn G, work same as Row 5.
Row 9: Attach yarn H, work same as Row 5.
Row 10: Attach yarn E, work same as Row 5.
Row 11: Attach yarn A. Ch 3 (counts as 1 dc). Starting in fifth ch from hook work 1 dc in each st. Turn. Fasten off.
Row 12: Attach yarn C, work same as Row 5.
Row 13: Attach yarn I, work same as Row 5.
Row 14: Attach yarn B, work same as Row 5.
Row 15: Attach yarn C, work same as Row 5, but do not fasten off. Turn.
Row 16: With yarn C, ch 2, starting with fourth ch from hook work 1 hdc in each st. Fasten off.

Lower Portion: With hook and yarn C, ch 67 sts. Work 1 row sc—66 sts. Turn.
Row 2: With yarn C, ch 2, work 1 hdc in same st, *sk next st, work 2 hdc in next st*; rep from * to * across row. Turn.
Row 3: With yarn C, ch 2, work 1 hdc in each st. Turn. Fasten off.
Rows 4–10: Work same as Row 2, working 1 row each of colors B, E, F, C, G, H, E.
Row 11: Attach yarn A. Ch 3, starting with fifth ch from hook work 1 dc in each st. Turn. Fasten off.
Row 12: Attach yarn C, work same as Row 2.
Row 13: Attach yarn I, work same as Row 2.
Row 14: Attach yarn B, work same as Row 2.
Row 15: Attach yarn C. Ch 3, starting with fifth ch from hook, work 1dc in each st. Turn.
Row 16: Continue with yarn C, work same as Row 2.
Rows 17–23: Work same as Rows 4–10.
Row 24: Work same as Row 11.
Rows 25–28: Work same as Rows 12–15.
Row 29: Work same as Row 2.
Rows 30–32: Work same as Rows 4–6.
Row 33: Attach yarn B, work 1 sc in each st. Fasten off.

FINISHING

With right sides of work together, pin pillow front to pillow back, making sure that buttonhole edge of back overlaps top of lower back portion. Slip-stitch crochet edges together all around, using edge stitches of pillow top as a guide and working through all three layers where necessary to overlap top portion of back. Remove pins. Turn pillow right side out. With threaded sewing needle, sew buttons opposite buttonholes. Insert pillow form adjusting as necessary for an even fit.

CROCHETING WITH NOVELTY YARNS

So many yarns can be classified as novelty that it is difficult to generalize about all the special effects they provide—and the challenges they pose. Novelty can refer to fiber content, such as rayon or nylon, or it can refer to metallic yarns that shine and sparkle. Novelty can also refer to yarn construction which adds a variety of effects with nubs, slubs, and eyelashes.

When you're working with a novelty yarn, consider its special features and properties and how they suit the project. Use stitches that will enhance these features and maximize their effect. For example, a yarn with large slubs needs a long stitch such as a double crochet to show it off. A single crochet stitch will not only hide the beauty of a slub yarn but will make it difficult to work with. Similarly, most ribbon yarns are used to best advantage in a long stitch that highlights their unique construction; ribbons tend to look like conventional yarns when they're worked tightly. An intricate stitch pattern will be lost or distorted if a slub yarn overshadows it. Not all novelty yarns are as durable as conventional yarns; therefore, they are often best used as trim rather than the primary yarn.

Consider a few special precautions when you're working with novelties. Shiny yarns, usually silk, nylon, or rayon, can be very slippery. Take care to keep tension consistent and to leave long ends (about 6" [15] cm) when you're changing colors. Weave these ends through more stitches than usual to secure them. To stop slippage, consider stitching down the ends with sewing thread after you weave them in. If there is a definite wrong side to the work that won't be visible when the finished piece is used, try to leave short lengths (½–1") [1.25–2.5 cm] of the ends sticking out after weaving rather than concealing them entirely or trimming them too close to the fabric. The extra length helps keep ends from popping through to the right side.

SNUGGLE UNDER

THROW

At once bold and graphic and warm and fuzzy, this is not your granny's afghan. Although its elements are made in traditional afghan form, the effect is mod.

SIZE

About 54" (137 cm) square.

YARN

Light bulky-weight mohair, about 2400 yd (2215 m). ***We used:*** Classic Elite La Gran mohair (76.5% mohair, 17.5% wool, 6% nylon; 90 yd [82 m]/42 g) 14 skeins #6513 black (A), 2 skeins each #6593 electric blue (E), #6526 tidal pool (D), #6555 infrared (B), 3 skeins #6572 underappreciated green (C), 4 skeins # 6511 seashell (F).

HOOK

Crochet hook size K/10½ (6.5 mm). Adjust hook size if necessary to obtain correct gauge.

NOTIONS

Tapestry needle, safety pins.

GAUGE

8 stitches and 8 rows = 3" (7.5 cm) in single crochet with size K/10½ (6.5 mm) hook.

ABBREVIATIONS

beg—beginning
ch—chain
dc—double crochet
rep—repeat
sc—single crochet
sl st—slip stitch
st (s)—stitch(es)

Review Basics, page 2:
Chain
Double crochet
Joining colors
Reading a pattern
Single crochet
Slip stitch
Weaving in ends

Note: The throw is made up of three different elements: large squares, small squares, and bordered by striped rectangles. See chart for color placement.

SMALL SQUARES

Make 25 small squares as follows: 16 color B, 8 color E, 1 color C. (All squares are edged with color A.)
Using hook and the appropriate color (either B, E, or C), ch 10 sts, turn. Starting in second ch from hook, work 1 sc in each ch for a total of 9 sc. Turn, working in same color, sc 8 more rows even—9 rows each with 9 sts. Fasten off as follows: Cut yarn leaving 4" (10 cm) tail, insert tail through last lp on hook and pull to tighten.

Attach color A to any corner. Work 1 sc in the same sp, work 8 more sc evenly along the edge. *Ch 2, working the first sc in same sp as the last st of previous side, work 8 more sc evenly along next side*; rep from * to * 2 more times. Ch 2, attach with sl st to first sc of first side. Fasten off.

STRIPED PANELS

Make 40 striped panels as follows: 4 panels in colors A and B, 8 in colors A and D, 12 in colors A and C, 16 in color A and F.
With Color A, ch 12, turn.
Row 1: Beg in second ch from hook, work 1 sc in each ch—11 sts.
Row 2: Ch 1, 11 sc.
Drop yarn but do not fasten off. *Attach appropriate color and work 2 rows sc. Drop yarn but do not fasten off*; pick up color A and rep from * to *. Alternate colors every 2 rows for a total of 22 rows, carrying the color not in use loosely up the side of work, end with 2 rows in Color A. Fasten off.

LARGE SQUARE PANELS

Make 16 total squares; refer to chart for color placement.
Center of Square: With color A, ch 9, turn. Starting in second ch from hook, work 1 sc in each ch-8 sc. Turn, ch 1, work 7 more rows in sc. Fasten off.
Rnd 1: Attach appropriate color at any corner, ch 3 (counts as 1 dc), work 7 dc evenly spaced along edge—8 dc, *ch 2 (does not count as st), working 1 dc in same sp as last dc of previous side, work 7 more dc evenly along next side—8 dc*; rep from * to * 2 more times, ch 2, attach with sl st to top of beg ch 3. Fasten off.
Rnd 2: Attach color A in any ch-2 sp, work 2 sc in same sp, *work 1 sc in each of next 8 sc, in ch-2 sp, work (2 sc, ch 2, 2 sc)*; rep from * to * 2 more times, work 1 sc in each of next 8 sc. In same sp as beg of round, work (2 sc, ch 2). Join with sl st to beg sc. Fasten off.
Rnd 3: Attach appropriate color in any ch-2 sp. Ch 3 (counts as 1 dc), work 1 dc in same sp, *work 1 dc in each of next 12 sc, in ch-2 sp work (2 dc, ch 2, 2 dc)*; rep from * to * 2 more times. Work 1 dc in each of next 12 sc. In same sp as beg ch and dc work (2 dc, ch 2), join with sl st to top of beg ch 3. Fasten off.
Rnd 4: Attach Color A in any ch-2 sp. Ch 3 (counts as 1 dc), work 1 dc in same sp, *work 1 dc in each of next 16 dc, in ch-2 sp work (2 dc, ch 2, 2 dc)*; rep from * to * 2 more times. Work 1 dc in each of next 16 dc. In same sp as beg ch 3 and dc, work (2 dc, ch 2), join with sl st to top of ch 3.

FINISHING

Following chart, using tapestry needle and Color A, slip-stitch the elements together. ***Hint:*** Sew small sections together, then join to form larger sections using safety pins to match edges.

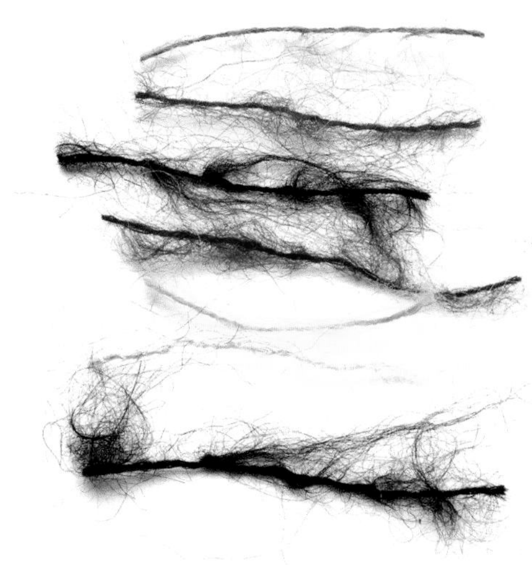

BORDER

Rnd 1: Attach color A at any corner, ch 3 (counts as 1 dc), work 1 dc in each of next 142 sts, ch 2 at corner, *work 1 dc in each of next 143 sts, ch 2* ; rep from * to * 2 more times. Join with sl st to top of beg ch 3. Fasten off.

Rnd 2: Attach color F to any ch-2 sp. Ch 3 (counts as 1 dc), work 1 dc in same sp, *work 1 dc in each dc to next corner, work (2 dc, ch 2, 2 dc)*; rep from * to * 2 more times, work 1 dc in each dc to next corner, (2 dc, ch 2) join with sl st to top of beg ch 3. Fasten off.

Rnd 3: Attach Color A and work same as for Rnd 2. Fasten off.

Rnd 4: (Picot Rnd, see page 79) Attach color C at any corner, *work 1 sc in each of next 3 sts, (ch 3, work 1 sl st in each of ch 2 just worked, and 1 sl st in last sc worked [picot made])*; rep from * to * around entire edge, working (2 sc, 1 picot, 2 sc) in corner ch-2 sp. Join with sl st to beg sc, fasten off.

Steam or block to afghan size and shape, and to smooth out seams.

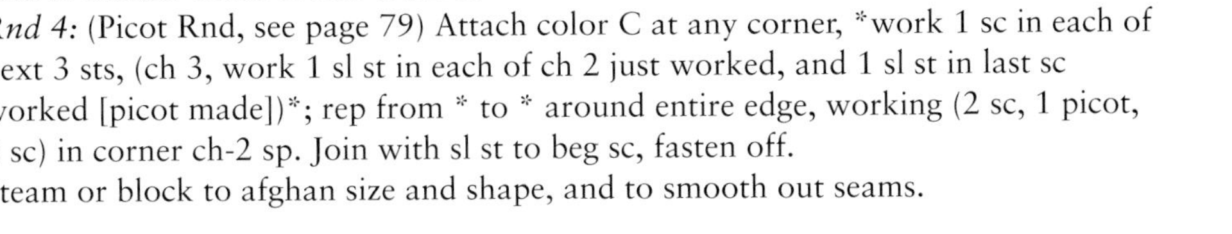

Color Placement Chart

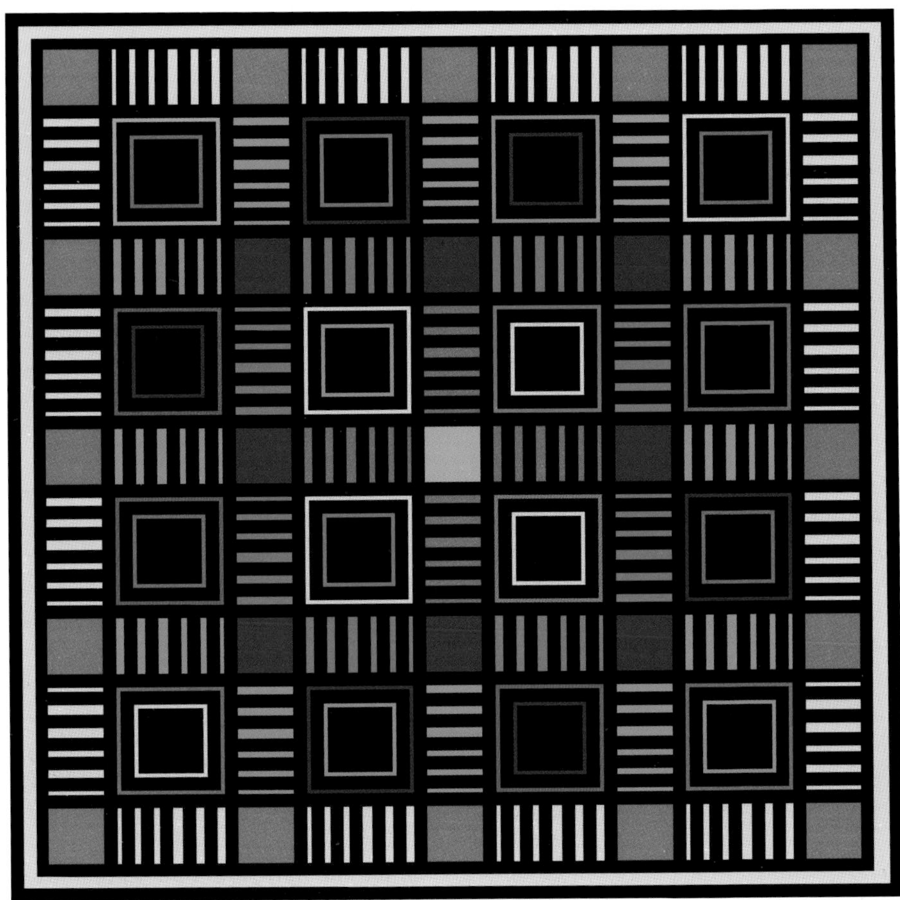

Apply final picot edging in C when throw is completely assembled as shown.

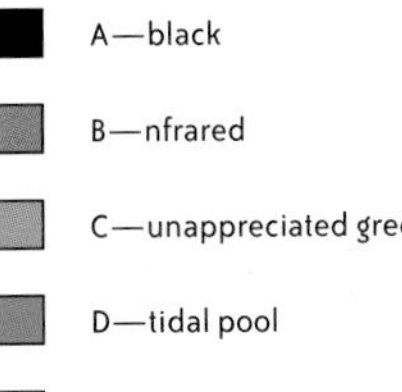

YARN SUPPLIERS

Generic yarn weights and approximate yardages are provided in the patterns so you can easily substitute any weight yarn you want. Contact the companies listed below if you don't have a local retailer or mail-order source for the yarns used in this book.

Berroco, Inc.
14 Elmdale Rd.
Uxbridge, MA 01569-0367
(508) 278-2527
In Canada, see S.R. Kertzer Ltd.
www.berroco.com

Brown Sheep Co., Inc.
10062 County Road 16
Mitchell, NE 69357
(308) 635-2198
www.brownsheep.com

Classic Elite Yarns
300 Jackson St.
Lowell, MA 01852
(800) 343-0308
In Canada, see S.R. Kertzer Ltd.

Dale of Norway
N 16 W 23390 Stoneridge Dr. Ste. A
Waukesha, WI 53188
(800) 387-DALE
www.dale.no

Diamond Yarn
155 Martin Ross, Unit 3
Toronto, ON M3J 2L9
Or
9697 St. Laurent, Ste. 101
Montreal QC H3L 2N1
www.diamondyarn.com

Jaeger, *see* Westminster Fibers

K1C2 (Knit One Crochet Too)
7 Commons Ave., Ste. 2
Windham, ME 04062
www.KnitOneCrochetToo.com

Knitting Fever/Jo Sharp
35 Debevoise Ave.
Roosevelt, NY 11575
(516) 546-3600
In Canada, see Diamond Yarn
www.knittingfever.com

Koigu Wool Designs
RR1
Williamsford, ON N0H 2V0
(888) 765-WOOL
www.koigu.com

Louet Sales/Gems
PO Box 267
808 Commerce Park Dr.
Ogdensburg, NY 13669
In Canada: R.R. 4, Prescott, ON K0E 1T0
www.louet.com

Rowan Yarns, *see* Westminster Fibers

Skacel Collection/Schoeller Esslinger
PO Box 88110
Seattle, WA 98136
(425) 291-9600
www.skacelknitting.com

S.R. Kertzer, Ltd.
105A Winges Rd.
Woodbridge, ON L4L 6C2
www.kertzer.com

Westminster Fibers
4 Townsend West, Unit 8
Nashua, NH 03063
(603) 886-5041
In Canada, see Diamond Yarn
www.knitrowan.com

INDEX